Name_____ Sport_____

Address_____

High School_____

Graduation Year_____

Club/AAU Team_____

Email_____

Phone #_____

Eligibility Center ID #_____

Date Started: _____ Date Completed:_____

College Recruiting Playbook

College Recruiting X's and O's

First Edition   **2015**

Christopher J. Stack

www.GuidingFutureStars.com

College Recruiting Playbook: College Recruiting X's and O's

By Christopher J. Stack

Credits: Cover: Lauren Noll Design. Design: Lauren Noll

Published by Create Space, DBA On-Demand Publishing, LLC

Charleston, SC

www.createspace.com

I want to thank the number of contributors to this project who have provided input into this project – friends, family, college coaches, parents, and young athletes.

Contributors:

TJ Burns	Denise Marjarum
Alexis Burns	Megan Molloy
Jill Calloway	Lindsey Munday
Jamion Christian	Paul Royal
Ryan Defibaugh	Darin Stull
Tom Gosselin	Greg White
Pat Horvath	Jessica Wolverton

College Recruiting Playbook: College Recruiting X's and O's

Copyright © 2015 by GFS Elite Marketing

All rights reserved. No part of this book may be reproduced or utilized in any form or by any means, electronic or mechanical, including photocopying, recording, or by any information storage or retrieval systems without permission in writing from the publisher.

Trademarks: All brand names and services used in this book are trademarks, registered trademarks, or trade names of their respective holders. Guiding Future Stars is not associated with any college, university, product, or vendor.

Printed in the United States of America

2 3 4 5 6 7 8 9 10

ISBN 978-0-9904426-0-8

LCCN 2014922515

"Guiding Future Stars to Gaining Future Success"

The GFS WAY

"Guiding Future Stars is committed to helping the next generation become excellent students, great athletes, and extraordinary people."

Vision

GFS is taking academic, athletic, and personal development to exciting new heights. We empower our student-athletes with the tools necessary to excel in the classroom, on the field, and in the community. Our ultimate goal is not only help prepare students for college but prepare them for the rest of their lives. Playing intercollege athletics is an experience that provides student-athletes with the opportunity to excel in a sport they love, while building an educational foundation for their future. Our approach, and our core values will help guide each of our prospective student-athletes towards finding the "right fit" as they navigate through the college recruiting process. The "right fit" means understanding what type of college experience the student-athlete is looking for and what is best for the family. We connect with each family's values and goals to create the best possible experience for the student-athlete throughout the college search process.

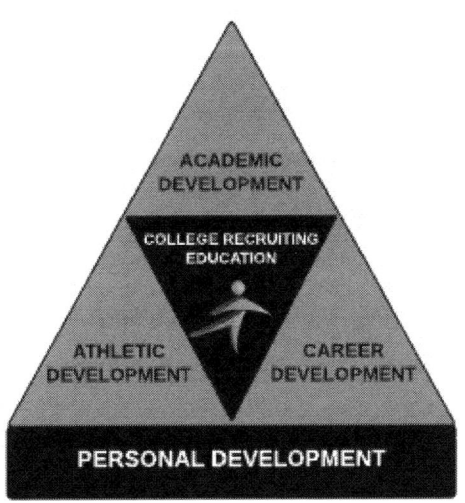

Come be a part of GFS, and maximize your <u>Potential</u>, your <u>Experiences</u>, and your <u>Community</u>

#GuidingFutureStars

TABLE OF CONTENTS

PHASE 1 PLANNING AND PREPARATION — 11

CHAPTER 1 BUILDING A COLLEGE LIST — 12
CHAPTER 2 NCAA ELIGIBILITY CENTER — 20
CHAPTER 3 NAVIGATING THE NCAA — 26
CHAPTER 4 LEVEL OF COMPETITION — 34
CHAPTER 5 PREPARING FOR THE SAT'S OR ACT'S — 37

PHASE 2 COMMUNICATION — 40

CHAPTER 6 WHAT COLLEGE COACHES WANT — 41
CHAPTER 7 INITIATING CONTACT — 50
CHAPTER 8 INITIAL CAMPUS VISIT — 55

PHASE 3 EXPOSURE — 59

CHAPTER 9 GAINING EXPOSURE — 60
CHAPTER 10 NARROWING YOUR LIST — 63
CHAPTER 11 THE OVERNIGHT VISIT — 65

PHASE 4 DECISION-MAKING — 66

CHAPTER 12 FINANCIAL AID — 67
CHAPTER 13 THE ADMISSION PROCESS — 72
CHAPTER 14 SELECTING THE RIGHT FIT — 75
CHAPTER 15 COMMITTING TO A SCHOOL — 77

PHASE 5 BEYOND THE DECISION — 80

CHAPTER 16 ACADEMIC PREPARATION — 81
CHAPTER 17 ATHLETIC PREPARATION — 82

APPENDICES — 83

APPENDIX I COLLEGE RECRUITING TIMELINE — 84
APPENDIX II GOAL SETTING — 88
APPENDIX III TIME MANAGEMENT — 90
APPENDIX IV WEIGHTED PROS CONS LIST — 92
APPENDIX V COLLEGE RECRUITING ORGANIZER — 95

RESOURCES/CONTRIBUTORS/REFERENCES — 157

Dear Prospective Student-Athlete,

Whether you are a student-athlete about to enter high school or you are well into your high school career, it's never too early or too late to think about playing sports in college. If you dream of playing sports in college then the College Recruiting Playbook is for you.

The College Recruiting Playbook is essential for student-athletes, this easy-to-read guide helps you identify the school that best fits you academically, athletically, and personally—so you can find success on *and off* the field. If you are committed to having a successful college sports career, you must take the initiative to make it happen.

The book is arranged by the 5 phases of the college recruiting process. By following the 5 phases of the college recruiting process you will increase your chances of finding the "right fit."

For a student-athlete, the college search process is a journey full of adventure. Be sure to explore all of your options so that you can make informed decisions. Do your homework and seek out the appropriate help to find the answers you need. It is your future. You're worth it!

We hope you find this publication helpful as you begin thinking about the rest of your life.

Sincerely,

Christopher J. Stack, President

Guiding Future Stars

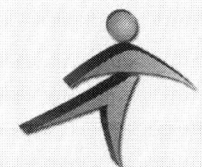

What is the College Recruiting Playbook?

Finding the right college for your student-athlete doesn't have to be complicated. In fact, with the *College Recruiting Playbook*, you can navigate the five phases of the recruiting process with surprising ease. This step-by-step guide walks parents and students through everything they need to know and do in order to find the best college academically, athletically, and personally.

GFS encourages you to begin thinking about the college process early. College coaches will begin evaluating prospective student-athletes online before anything else. As you learn how the process works behind the scenes, you can begin to form your own game plan, promoting your teen's athletic achievements to successfully attract the coaches and schools you both want.

Written especially for high school athletes, this guide is also an essential read for parents, teachers, and coaches. By utilizing the included organizer and looking at the process from more than an athlete's point of view, you can form the best strategy for your young athlete's near and distant future.

5 PHASES OF THE COLLEGE RECRUITING PROCESS

- Planning and Preparation
- Communication
- Gaining Exposure
- Decision Making
- Beyond the Decision

The College Recruiting Playbook will guide you through everything you need to know and everything you need to do to find a college where you will develop academically, athletically, and personally.

College Recruiting Process Snapshot

4 Things you need to know

- Recruiting process starts early
- Being identified by college coaches does not happen magically
- College coaches will begin evaluating prospects online
- Be Realistic

4 Things you need to do

- Begin with the End in Mind
- Develop a Game Plan
- Create a customized marketing plan
- Contact Coaches. Visit Schools

Features of the Book

Essential for student-athletes, this easy-to-read guide helps you identify the school that best fits you academically, personally, and athletically—so you can find success on *and* off the field. By understanding the features included in the book students can preview the topics and strategies that will be used in each chapter.

SELF-ASSESSMENTS

The self-assessments will assist prospective student-athletes in discovering the values that are important to them in their recruiting process.

TABLES

The tables are used to help prospective student-athletes organize pertinent information as they navigate through the college recruiting process.

RECRUITING CHARTS

The recruiting charts are used to show prospective student-athletes academic standards and the NCAA Recruiting Rules recruits should know in order to navigate through the recruiting process.

RECRUITING TERMS

The recruiting terms are essential for prospective student-athletes to understand as they navigate through the college recruiting process.

GFS TIPS

The GFS Tips appear as boxed inserts in each chapter. These are useful tips to help you throughout the college recruiting process.

REVIEW IT

This section tests your knowledge of what you learned in the chapter.

APPENDIX

The appendix includes a number of resources that prospective student-athletes can utilize before, during, and after the recruiting process. The College Recruiting Organizer will help you manage and organize your entire college recruiting process.

PARENTS EXPECTATIONS IN THE RECRUITING PROCESS

Parents should focus on what is right for their son or daughter. Don't push them in a direction they don't want to go or are not a good fit for. Remember college coaches are recruiting your child, not you. You should help your child work through this book and provide them with guidance and support.

- Be respectful of your son or daughter's ownership of the college admissions decision-making process. It is the student who will spend the years on the college campus, and therefore, the decision must ultimately be theirs. Students can gain decision-making skills, improve their self- confidence, and develop perseverance which will help them throughout their lives.

- Be realistic regarding your child's abilities and talents. While each student is special and has unique qualities, it is difficult for a parent to be entirely objective about one's own child! Remember that college admissions are extremely competitive (especially within state) and there are many talented young people.

- Give your son or daughter the benefit of your wisdom and your experience, and tell the student "up front" if there will be restrictions (financial or otherwise) on his/her college options.

- Remember, the student wants and needs your help in the process but does not need to be overwhelmed with your impressions and ideas. Be available to help when help is solicited.

- Help with some of the logistical aspects of the college-search process. Plan travel arrangements to campuses, schedule college interviews (where available), and schedule testing. Help to ensure that critical deadlines are met. Be supportive of your child's aspirations, but encourage him/her to be realistic. Help him/her to select the "best" college choices, not necessarily the "top-name" or most prestigious institution.

- Prepare your child to be an independent being. Encourage time away from home where your child must be self-reliant. Help establish a checking account, and help your child learn to do his/her laundry.

- Realize that the college admissions process is a highly stressful time for the students as well as the parent. Take each part of the process one step at a time, and remember that help is always readily available.

- Prepare for the transition to college. The summer after high school graduation, as well as the first semester of college, can be difficult periods. As your son or daughter makes the adjustment from high school to college, avoid over-reacting to new situations; try to sort through the conflicts and issues as they arise.

PROSPECTIVE STUDENT-ATHLETE EXPECTATIONS IN THE RECRUITING PROCESS

The college recruiting process is an exciting time for a high school student-athlete. Make sure you are looking for the "right fit" for you and nobody else.

- Be true to yourself. While you should listen carefully to the advice of others, avoid being overly swayed by peer pressure or the impressions of others.

- Begin the college search process early, allowing plenty of time to gather information, to think about your decisions, and to process the paperwork.

- Visit the schools to which you are most interested in. There is no substitute for seeing the college and getting the feel for the "campus"

- Apply to colleges of varying selectivity standards. Have at least one safety colleges on your list. While it is okay to apply to one or two "reach" colleges, be realistic – are the colleges within the range of possibility?

- Remember, a deadline is a deadline is a deadline. Plot your deadlines on your calendar and establish a workable plan for completing the applications in plenty of time. Allow for unexpected complications at the last moment. Be sure to note if the college's deadline is a "due there by" or "postmark by" deadline if you are applying via U.S. Mail.

- Don't let the process get you down. Keep in mind that thousands of other students are applying to college along with you and that others share your fears and concerns. Find positive ways to relieve your stress, and don't hesitate to ask for help when needed. Support your classmates, and they will support you

- It is important to keep everything organized and maintain complete and accurate records!

START PLANNING YOUR FUTURE TODAY!

Are you looking for some assistance with your college search? Let GFS help you create a game plan to achieve your goal of playing in college.

Visit http://www.guidingfuturestars.com/Prospective-Student-Athlete.html and fill out the student-athlete questionnaire.

MESSAGE FROM THE AUTHOR

"If you have a goal then you should do something every day to achieve it."

I grew up in the suburbs just outside of Philadelphia, PA. I played just about every sport growing up from golf to street hockey to soccer. Soccer was my true passion. I started playing at five years old - running up and down the field at Shady Grove Elementary School on Saturday morning's scoring lots of goals. As I grew and my skills progressed, I started playing soccer on an increasingly competitive level. This allowed me the opportunity to travel around the country and play in national level competitions. My parents' parent's made a lot of sacrifices to give me that opportunity and I will be forever grateful to them.

By the age of 14 I knew I wanted to play soccer in college. Growing up in the 90's every kid who played soccer dreamed of playing at the University of Virginia (UVA) - I was no exception. The UVA Men's Soccer program was a dynasty! They had won four consecutive national championships from 1991 to 1994. I envisioned one day having the opportunity to put on a UVA jersey and play at the famous Klockner Stadium, home of former U.S. National Soccer Team stars John Harkes and Claudio Reyna. As I entered high school, I continued to work on developing my skill set. My club team at the time, was one of the best in Pennsylvania. In 1995, we won the Eastern Pennsylvania Youth Soccer Association State Cup and advanced to the Region I Finals in Buffalo, New York. Though we lost in the semi-finals it was a great experience. During my sophomore year of high school, I had several injuries which caused setbacks in my game. I realized, at this time, that I didn't have the talent needed to play for an elite program such as UVA. I was disappointed at first but I did not let it deter me from my goal - playing college soccer.

During my senior year of high school, I was on the Varsity team, but I saw very little playing time. And without a club team or lots of varsity play time being scouted by a college coach was very difficult. Luckily, I did not give up. I reached out to a number of schools and college coaches at the DI and DIII levels. I was looking at colleges that would be the right fit for me - both academically and personally. This process was really hard for me to navigate. I felt like there was no one to help. After contacting several different coaches I had no guarantees that I would play. In December, 1997, I received my acceptance letter to Mount St. Mary's College and immediately contacted the head coach about walking on to the soccer team. Unfortunately, he said that his roster was full and there was no room for me. Coach added me to the reserve team and said that, if I worked hard, this could lead to a roster spot in the spring of my freshmen year. The reserve team was coached by an assistant coach of the men's team so there was a direct connection to the Varsity squad. I began my freshmen year playing on the reserve team, only practicing twice a week, but I knew that wasn't enough to improve my skills. I organized small group sessions with some of my fellow reserve players who had the same aspirations of making the varsity team. In order to be successful I had to be committed to getting better and I had to do it on my own. I spent countless hours running, working out, and improving my technical skills so that when the time came I could make an impression on the head coach. As the spring rolled around I got an invitation from the head coach to have a two month trial with the varsity team. After my two month trial, the head coach offered me a spot on the team for the 1999-2000 season. Fortunately, my hard work and dedication paid off.

On September 15, 1999 my dream of playing soccer at UVA came true. The Mount travelled to Charlottesville, VA to take on the nationally ranked Cavaliers. I had my chance to play against UVA at the famous Klockner Stadium and it was a night I will never forget. My dream to one day play for the University of Virginia didn't quite pan out as I had hoped, but I still got to play on that storied field. What an experience that was!

Overall, people may say that I had a mediocre college career: playing in 23 games, making 12 starts in 3 years, but it was an experience that I will always remember; I would not change it for the world. Soccer was only one part of my college experience. It's the lifelong friends and memories that I made while I was there that will last forever.

I wrote this guide for two reasons: First, to let you know that you can achieve anything you put your mind to. If you really want to do something you have to make it happen. Second, to inform, educate, guide, and inspire young student-athletes to go out and chase their dreams. The college recruiting process can be a very daunting, but if you have a plan and take it a step at a time it will be an amazing experience. You will learn a lot about who you are and what you can achieve if you are willing to step up to the challenge.

I would consider myself a living "Rudy," the famous movie about a football player who walked onto the Notre Dame Football team from nowhere. Don't let anybody tell you that you can't do something. If you really want something work hard and prove people wrong. That's what I did.

– Christopher J. Stack

Begin with the End in Mind

Dr. Steven Covey, famous author of the *7 Habits of Highly Effective People* was renowned for working with presidents, CEO's, athletes, and teachers. Stephen taught the mindset, skillset and toolset found in the *7 habits of Highly Effective People*. The 2nd habit is Begin with the End in Mind. Begin with the End in Mind means to begin each day, task, or project with a clear vision of your desired direction and destination, and then continue by flexing your proactive muscles to make things happen. I believe this habit is important when you begin your college recruiting process. Choosing a college is one of the biggest decisions a teenager will make in their life. And making this decision is one of the first steps to adulthood. Selecting a college is more than deciding where you are going to spend the next four years of your life, it's about becoming the person you want to be after you graduate. Attending college is all about development of one's self. And as a student-athlete you want to find a place where you will develop in the classroom, on the field, and in the community.

When you begin the college recruiting process you should look at it from three perspectives.

- You as a student
- You as an athlete
- You as a young man or women

And then answer this question. Where will I develop the most in those three aspects of my life?

We will begin the recruiting process by asking you to look into your future. What do you want to get out of your college experience? Where do you see yourself after college? Answering these questions will help you figure out how your college experience will help shape you into the person you want to be in 5, 10, or 20 years down the road.

Self-Assessment 1 – 1

Why do you want to go to college? Do you want to play a sport in college? And if yes, why?

_____
_____
_____
_____
_____
_____
_____
_____
_____

Take a few minutes to write about what you are looking for in your college experience.
Discuss factors like location, size, major, social environment, and athletic experience.
BE SPECIFIC

_____
_____
_____
_____
_____
_____
_____
_____

Where do you see yourself a year after you graduate? How do you want to be remembered?

_____
_____
_____
_____
_____
_____
_____
_____

PHASE 1

PLANNING AND PREPARATION:
Creating your Recruiting Game Plan

"PLANNING IS BRINGING THE FUTURE INTO THE PRESENT SO THAT YOU CAN DO SOMETIHNG ABOUT IT NOW"

- Alan Lakein, writer

OBJECTIVES

- CHAPTER 1 BUILDING A COLLEGE LIST
- CHAPTER 2 NCAA ELIGIBILITY CENTER
- CHAPTER 3 NAVIGATING THE NCAA
- CHAPTER 4 LEVEL OF COMPETITION
- CHAPTER 5 PREPARING FOR SATS

CHAPTER 1 BUILDING A COLLEGE LIST

High school student-athletes are encouraged to build a balanced list of colleges. But what does that mean? When creating your initial list of colleges don't limit yourself by narrowing your preferences down too much too soon. You should keep an open mind until you begin visiting campuses. A balanced list of colleges should include 20 – 30 schools made up of 3 categories. Each category can be related to either the students' academic or athletic profile or both.

- **"Safe" School** - The students' profile is significantly stronger than most of the students admitted.
- **"Target" School** - The students' profile is similar to most of the students admitted.
- **"Reach" School** - The students' profile is not as strong as most of the students admitted.

What kind of college experience are you looking for? There are many factors to consider when you begin building your initial list of colleges. Here are some questions to ponder as you begin your college recruiting process. Please consider how important each of these factors are to your college experience.

TYPES OF COLLEGES

- Do you want to go to a two-year college? At a two year college you can earn an Associate's Degree and then transfer to a four-year college.
- Do you have a preference of whether you attend a public college or a private college? The myth is that private schools are more expensive than public schools but that is not always the case. Financial Aid from private schools can sometimes make it as affordable as public universities
- Are you looking for a specific religious affiliation?

GEOGRAPHICAL LOCATION OF COLLEGES

- In what part of the country do you want to go to school? What kind of climate do you want to go to school in?
- How far away do you want to be from your home? Do you want to be a car ride away, or are you willing to go as far as a plane ride? Do you want your parents to come see you play as much as possible?

CAMPUS SETTING

- Do you want to go to a big state school or attend a smaller liberal arts college?
- Do you want a very diverse college, or do you want to be around students with similar interests and backgrounds?
- Do you want to go to school in a big city, suburbs, or in a small college town?

COST

- What do you know about college costs? Students do not generally pay the published tuition costs because of different forms of financial aid.
- Will I qualify for financial aid? All students should fill out a Free Application For Student-Aid (FAFSA)
- What scholarships am I eligible for? Are there Merit or Academic Scholarships available?

LEARNING ENVIRONMENT

- Do you want to be academically challenged or academically comfortable? Are you interested in attending Ivy League or Patriot League School? Are you interested in attending a Service Academy?
- Are you interested in being able to interact with your professors or attend classes in large lecture halls?
- What kind of balance are you looking for between academics, athletics, and your social life?

LEVEL OF COMPETITION

Do you want to play Division I, II, III, or NAIA? The NCAA has a maximum number of scholarships allowed for each sport.

THE ATHLETIC PROGRAM

- What Division is the program?
- What Conference does the school belong to?
- Who is the coach? Who are the assistants? How long have they been there?
- What type of facilities do they have?
- What does the current roster look like? Is there a lot of turnover from year to year?
- How many graduating seniors are there?
- What is the academic success of the team?
- Is it a winning program? Do you want to go to a winning program? Do you want to be a part of a program that is rebuilding?

OTHER FACTORS TO CONSIDER

- The retention and graduation rates
- Admission standards
- The employment rates for graduates
- Career services available
- Average debt upon graduation
- Campus Safety
- Internship opportunities
- Academic services
- Retention efforts/student advising
- Most popular student events

- The wider you cast your net looking for the right college, the more you will find. Don't fixate on "big name" schools – search high and low for the right college fit.

- Know Yourself! Keep your personal preferences in mind. If you know a large school with large lecture halls will not suit you then keep them off your list. Or if you want to go to a school in warmer climate then don't search for schools in the north.

- Research colleges and get a feel for the different types of campuses. Evaluate a wide range of schools, and understand that bigger is not always better. Division I schools do not always offer better playing time, opportunities, or education than Division III or NAIA schools.

- Research, research, research. Determining your best-fit school involves much more than just deciding which college you like the most. Not every school you're interested in will have a need for a student-athlete of your caliber or at your position, so you need to study and contact as many schools and coaches as you can to determine which one is best for you.

- Visit local colleges. Take the opportunity to visit schools in the surrounding area even if you are not interested. You can get a feel for large campuses or smaller schools. You can see what city schools are like or schools in college towns. Try and visit a Division I school and compare it to a Division II or III school.

- Discuss finances with your parents. If there are financial expectations discuss that with your parents before you get too far into the process. Be sure to look at net cost rather than tuition. It is very rare that students pay full price at any institution.

Brown, Kerry (2012) *"Top 50 Recruiting Tips* – NCSA Athletic Recruiting Blog

Self-Assessment 1 – 2

Rate the following factors on how important they are to your college search. Use a 1 – 10, with 1 being the most important factor in your college search.

Type of College	_____	Size/Enrollment	_____
Geographical Location	_____	Level of competition	_____
Campus Setting	_____	The Athletic Program	_____
Cost	_____	Academic Standards	_____
Learning Environment	_____	Graduation Rates	_____

Now that you have rated the factors that are most important to you in your college search it is time to answer questions about those factors and build your college list.

KINDS OF COLLEGES - CIRCLE ONE ANSWER

Which college do you prefer?   2 Year College   4 Year College

Which college do you prefer?   Private   Public   No Preference

Are you looking for a specific religious affiliation?   Yes   No

If Yes, what religious affiliation _____

GEOGRAPHICAL LOCATION – CIRCLE ALL THAT APPLY

Where would you like to attend college?   Mid-Atlantic   Northeast   Southeast   Midwest   Southwest   West Coast   No Preference

How many miles away from home do you want to travel?   1-49   50-100   100-200   200 +   No preference

CAMPUS SETTING – CIRCLE ALL THAT APPLY

What size school would you like to attend?   Small (Less than 3,000)   Medium (3,000-8,000)   Large (8,000 – 15,000)   Very Large (15,000 +)

What campus setting are you looking for?   Rural   College Town   Suburb   Urban   No Preference

ACADEMIC PROGRAMS

Do you know what you would like to major in?   Yes   Undecided

If yes, what would it be? _____

Are you interested in studying at a Liberal Arts Institution?   Yes   No   No Preference

COST

Are you looking for an athletic scholarship?   Yes   No   No Preference

Do you plan on taking out a college loan?   Yes   No

What is the maximum amount you are willing to pay for college? (optional) _____

LEARNING ENVIRONMENT

Do you want to be academically challenged? Yes   No

Do you want to be academically comfortable?   Yes   No

Do you want smaller class sizes?   Yes   No

Do you want large lecture halls?   Yes   No

What kind of balance are you looking for between academics, athletics, and social life? Explain.

_____

LEVEL OF COMPETITION – CIRCLE ALL THAT APPLY

What Division do you want to play at?   DI   DII   DIII   NAIA   No Preference

Having answered these questions you should have a better idea of the academic, athletic, and social environment that's right for you. How do you find schools that fit your criteria?

Researching schools is very time consuming but also very necessary to the recruiting process. You need to learn as much information about a school before you add it to your list. You should talk to your parents, guidance counselors, coaches, and former teammates about the schools that interest you. In addition you should utilize the internet for gathering information and watching videos.

Here are some excellent resources to utilize as you navigate through the college recruiting process.

Here are a few other college search engines to assist you in seeking information
- **College View**: www.collegeview.com
- **College Data**: www.collegedata.com
- **Peterson's**: www.petersons.com/college-search.aspx
- **Princeton Review**: www.princetonreview.com/schoolsearch.aspx

- **College Board:** www.collegeboard.org
  The College Board is the Official Website for the SAT's. Every high school student who plans to take the SATs should create a College Board Account. You can register for the SATs, manage your scores, and much more. College Board also has its own college search tool where you can narrow your list using a number of different criteria.
  https://bigfuture.collegeboard.org/college-search

- **National Center for Education Statistics:** http://nces.ed.gov/collegenaviagator/
  The NCES is a great resource to find college profiles that includes all of the pertinent information you are looking for about a school including location, setting, enrollment, tuition, net cost, and student to faculty ratio, just to name a few.

Exercise 1-1: Build Your College List

Utilizing the college search resources you have at your disposal, create an initial list of schools that fit the college experience you are looking for. This list is just a starting point until you get a better idea of what kinds of things you are look for in a college.

Using the tables on the following pages, make a list of schools that you are interested in.

> Column 1 – Name of the College
>
> Column 2 – Type: Is the College Public or Private
>
> Column 3 – Location: The city in which the college or university is located
>
> Column 4 – Setting: Is the campus in a rural, college town, suburb, or city
>
> Column 5 – Cost: What is the published tuition (Total Cost; Tuition, Room, and Board)
>
> Column 6 – AVG NC: What is the average net cost of the college?
>
> Column 7 – Size: What is the undergraduate enrollment?
>
> Column 8 – Student: Faculty Ratio
>
> Column 9 – Div.: What division is the school? DI, DII, DIII, NAIA, or NJCAA
>
> Column 10- Conference: What conference is the school in? (e.g. Big Ten, ACC, SEC, etc)

Recruiting Notes

_____

_____

_____

_____

_____

_____

_____

Table 1 – 1 My Colleges

COLLEGE	TYPE	LOCATION	SETTING	COST	AVG NC	SIZE	STUD:FAC RATIO	DIV.	CONFERENCE
1.									
2.									
3.									
4.									
5.									
6.									
7.									
8.									
9.									
10.									
11.									
12.									
13.									
14.									

COLLEGE	TYPE	LOCATION	SETTING	COST	AVG NC	SIZE	STUD:FAC RATIO	DIV.	CONFERENCE
15.									
16.									
17.									
18.									
19.									
20.									
21.									
22.									
23.									
24.									
25.									
26.									
27.									
28.									

CHAPTER 2 NCAA ELIGIBILITY CENTER

If you wish to participate in NCAA Division I or II athletics, you need to be certified by the NCAA Eligibility Center. You need to qualify academically and you will also need to be cleared as an amateur student-athlete. You are responsible for achieving and protecting your eligibility status!

About the NCAA Eligibility Center
Student-athletes must register with the NCAA Eligibility Center to be eligible to play NCAA Division I or II sports in college. Athletes playing in Division III do not have to register.

What is the NCAA Eligibility Center?
The NCAA Eligibility Center certifies whether prospective college athletes are eligible to play sports at NCAA Division I or II institutions. It does this by reviewing the student-athlete's academic record, test scores, and amateur status to ensure conformity with NCAA rules.

When should students register?
The NCAA recommends that student-athletes register at the **beginning of their junior year** in high school, but many students register after their junior year. There is no registration deadline, but students must be cleared by the Eligibility Center before they receive athletic scholarships or compete at a Division I or II institution.

How do students register?
Students must register online at the NCAA Eligibility Center. They will have to enter personal information, answer questions about their course work and sports participation outside of high school and pay a registration fee. www.eligibilitycenter.org

Can students have the registration fee waived?
Students who have received a waiver for the SAT or ACT are eligible for a waiver of the registration fee. The student's counselor must submit confirmation of the student's test fee waiver. Go to the NCAA Eligibility Center High School Portal for more information.

What records does the Eligibility Center require?
Students should arrange to send their high school transcript as soon as they have completed at least six semesters of high school. The transcript must be mailed directly from their high school. They must also arrange to have their SAT or ACT test scores reported directly by the testing company to the Eligibility Center. Students can arrange this when they register for the tests.

How often can students update their athletics participation information?
Students can update the information on the athletics participation section online as often as they want (and should update it regularly), up until the time when they request a final certification of their status. At that point — usually three to four months before enrolling in college — students must finalize their information.

What are the NCAA academic eligibility requirements?
To play sports at an NCAA Division I or II institution, the student must:
- Complete a certain number of high school core courses.
- Earn a certain minimum grade point average in these core courses.
- Earn a certain minimum score on the SAT or ACT.
- Graduate from high school.

What are core courses?
This is the name that the NCAA gives to high school courses that meet certain academic criteria specified by the association. Students must complete a certain number of core courses for NCAA Division I and II eligibility. Please see the Core Course Worksheets on pages 24 and 25.

How are high school courses classified as core courses?
All participating high schools submit lists of the courses that they offer that meet NCAA core-course criteria. If approved, the courses are added to a database that the NCAA Eligibility Center maintains. You can check this database or view a list of approved core courses on the NCAA Eligibility Center High School Portal to see whether you are enrolled in courses that will count toward NCAA eligibility. It is often the counselor who provides the NCAA with the list of your school's core courses and updates it annually. The NCAA may ask for more information before approving a core course.

What are the NCAA amateurism eligibility requirements?
To play sports at an NCAA Division I or II institution, the student athlete must follow NCAA amateurism rules about receiving a salary or prize money for athletic participation, playing with a professional team and other areas.

Keep in mind the best way for students to prepare for a future in college athletics is to complete the approved core courses and earn appropriate grades in them. Indeed, more students fail to qualify to play NCAA sports because of lack of appropriate course work than for low test scores.

Have you registered with the NCAA Eligibility Center?   Yes   No   Attend DIII or NAIA school.

If yes, what is your ID Number? _____

NEW ELIGIBILITY REQUIREMENTS BEGINNING FOR CLASS OF 2016

Incoming student-athletes must present a grade point average that predicts academic success at the collegiate level.

- Beginning August 1, 2016 you must earn at least a 2.30 GPA in NCAA core courses to be eligible to compete in your first year of college.
- To get a scholarship and practice you must earn at least a 2.00 GPA in NCAA core courses.
- Only courses that appear on your high school's list of NCAA courses will be used to calculate your GPA for NCAA eligibility purposes. For a complete list of your school's courses, visit www.eligibilitycenter.org.
- Once ten core courses are "locked in" prior to the start of your seventh semester, you can't take those classes over again to improve your GPA.
- Division I uses a sliding scale to match test scores and core GPA's.

Recruiting Chart 2 – 1 NCAA Eligibility Center Rolling Scale

	Use for Division I prior to August 1, 2016			Use for Division I beginning August 1, 2016	
Core GPA	SAT	ACT	Core GPA	SAT	ACT
3.550 & above	400	37	3.550 & above	400	37
3.525	410	38	3.525	410	38
3.500	420	39	3.500	420	39
3.475	430	40	3.475	430	40
3.450	440	41	3.450	440	41
3.425	450	41	3.425	450	41
3.400	460	42	3.400	460	42
3.375	470	42	3.375	470	42
3.350	480	43	3.350	480	43
3.325	490	44	3.325	490	44
3.300	500	44	3.300	500	44
3.275	510	45	3.275	510	45
3.250	520	46	3.250	520	46
3.225	530	46	3.225	530	46
3.200	540	47	3.200	540	47
3.175	550	47	3.175	550	47
3.150	560	48	3.150	560	48
3.125	570	49	3.125	570	49
3.100	580	49	3.100	580	49
3.075	590	50	3.075	590	50
3.050	600	50	3.050	600	50
3.025	610	51	3.025	610	51
3.000	620	52	3.000	620	52
2.975	630	52	2.975	630	52
2.950	640	53	2.950	640	53
2.925	650	53	2.925	650	53
2.900	660	54	2.900	660	54
2.875	670	55	2.875	670	55
2.850	680	56	2.850	680	56
2.825	690	56	2.825	690	56
2.800	700	57	2.800	700	57
2.775	710	58	2.775	710	58
2.750	720	59	2.750	720	59
2.725	730	59	2.725	730	60
2.700	730	60	2.700	740	61
2.675	740-750	61	2.675	750	61
2.650	760	62	2.650	760	62
2.625	770	63	2.625	770	63
2.600	780	64	2.600	780	64
2.575	790	65	2.575	790	65
2.550	800	66	2.550	800	66
2.525	810	67	2.525	810	67
2.500	820	68	2.500	820	68
2.475	830	69	2.475	830	69

2.450	840-850	70	2.450	840	70	
2.425	860	70	2.425	850	70	
2.400	860	71	2.400	860	71	
2.375	870	72	2.375	870	72	
2.350	880	73	2.350	880	73	
2.325	890	74	2.325	890	74	
2.300	900	75	**2.300**	**900**	**75**	
2.275	910	76	2.299	910	76	
2.250	920	77	2.275	910	76	
2.225	930	78	2.250	920	77	
2.200	940	79	2.225	930	78	
2.175	950	80	2.200	940	79	
2.150	960	80	2.175	950	80	
2.125	960	81	2.150	960	81	
2.100	970	82	2.125	970	82	
2.075	980	83	2.100	980	83	
2.050	990	84	2.075	990	84	
2.025	1000	85	2.050	1000	85	
2.000	**1010**	**86**	2.025	1010	86	
			2.000	1020	86	

NATIONAL ASSOCIATION OF INTERCOLLEGIATE ATHLETICS (NAIA)

The NAIA has different eligibility requirements for student-athletes. To be eligible to participate in intercollegiate athletics as an incoming freshmen, two of the following three requirements must be met:

1. Have a 2.0, C or higher cumulative final grade point average in high school.

2. Have a composite score of 18 or higher on the ACT Assessment or an 860 total score or higher on the SAT I on a single test administered on a national test date.

3. Have a top-half final class rank in his or her high school graduating class.

DO YOU WANT TO BE A FUTURE STAR?

Do you need help finding the right college to fit your academic, athletic, and personal needs? Let GFS help you navigate through the college recruiting process.

Check out http://www.guidingfuturestars.com/Future-Star.html and see what GFS has to offer.

Recruiting Chart 2 – 2 NCAA CORE COURSE DIVISION I WORKSHEET

A = 4 quality points; B= 3 quality points; C = 2 quality points; D= 1 quality point.

COURSE TITLE	CREDIT	GRADE	QUALITY POINTS (multiply credit by grade)
English – 4 Years required			
Fr.			
So.			
Jr.			
Sr.			
Total English Units			Total Quality Points
Mathematics – 3 years required			
1.			
2.			
3.			
Total Mathematics Units			Total Quality Points
Natural/Physical Science – 2 years			
1.			
2.			
Total Natural/Physical Science Units			Total Quality Points
Additional Year in English, Math, or Natural/Physical Science			
1.			
Total Additional Units			Total Quality Points
Social Science – 2 Years required			
1.			
2.			
Total Social Science Units			Total Quality Points
Additional Academic Courses – 4 Years required			
1.			
2.			
3.			
4.			
Total Additional Academic Units			Total Quality Points
Core Course GPA (16 required) Beginning August 1, 2016, 10 core courses to be completed prior to the Seventh semester and seven of the 10 must be a combination of English, Math, Natural or Physical Science.			
Total Quality Points	Total Number of Credits		Core-Course GPA (Total Quality Points/Total Credits

Recruiting Chart 2 – 3 NCAA CORE COURSE DIVISION II WORKSHEET

A = 4 quality points; B= 3 quality points; C = 2 quality points; D= 1 quality point.

COURSE TITLE	CREDIT	GRADE	QUALITY POINTS (multiply credit by grade)
English – 3 Years required			
Fr.			
So.			
Jr.			
Sr.			
Total English Units			Total Quality Points
Mathematics – 2 years required			
1.			
2.			
Total Mathematics Units			Total Quality Points
Natural/Physical Science – 2 years			
1.			
2.			
Total Natural/Physical Science Units			Total Quality Points
Additional Years in English, Math, or Natural/Physical Science – 3 Years required			
1.			
2.			
3.			
Total Additional Units			Total Quality Points
Social Science – 2 Years required			
1.			
2.			
Total Social Science Units			Total Quality Points
Additional Academic Courses – 4 Years required			
1.			
2.			
3.			
4.			
Total Additional Academic Units			Total Quality Points
Core Course GPA (16 required			
Total Quality Points	Total Number of Credits		Core-Course GPA (Total Quality Points/Total Credits

CHAPTER 3 NAVIGATING THE NCAA

What is the NCAA?

The National Collegiate Athletic Association (NCAA) is the governing body of many intercollegiate sports. Each college regulated by the NCAA has established rules on eligibility, recruiting and financial aid and falls into one of the three membership divisions (Divisions I, II and III). Divisions are based on college size and the scope of their athletic programs and scholarships.

What is the NAIA?

The National Association of Intercollegiate Athletics (NAIA) is an athletic association that organizes college and university-level athletic programs. Membership in the NAIA consists of smaller colleges and universities across the United States. Many of the NAIA schools are found in the Southeast, Midwest, and West Coast of the United States.

NCAA RECRUITING RULES OVERVIEW

Prospective Student-Athlete

You become a "prospective student athlete" when

- You start ninth-grade
- Before your ninth grade year, a college gives you, your relatives or your friends any financial assistance or other benefits that the college does not normally provide to students generally.

Recruited Prospective Student-Athlete

A prospective student-athlete becomes a recruited prospective student-athlete when any one of the following occur:

- A coach provides you with an official visit
- A coach places more than one phone call to you or any family member
- A coach visits you anywhere other than the institution's campus

Recruiting Periods

- **Contact Period:** This is the time when NCAA allows personal off-campus contact between a coach and a PSA
- **Quiet Period:** Coaches cannot recruit off campus but they can communicate via phone calls and in writing
- **Dead Period:** NCAA does not permit any contact at all between a coach and a PSA

Contacts

The NCAA considers a contact any off campus interaction with a college coach that is more than a friendly greeting. A college coach is prohibited from any contacts before a PSA's senior year. NCAA Division I coaches are permitted three off campus contacts with a PSA.

Evaluation

The NCAA describes an evaluation as any off-campus activity designed to assess the academic or athletic ability of the prospective student-athlete. A coach can evaluate a PSA a maximum of seven times prior to signing a National Letter of Intent.

Phone Calls

PSA's cannot receive phone calls from an NCAA Division I college coach until September 1 of their junior year. At that point a college coach may call a PSA once a week.

Variations to the Rule

- A football PSA can receive one phone call in May of his junior year from any institution.
- A men's basketball player can receive one phone call per month from June 15 prior to his junior year until June 30 prior to his senior year.
- A women's basketball player can receive one phone call in April and one phone call in May of her junior year.

NCAA Division II

- A coach can initiate a phone call prior to June 15 prior to the PSA's junior year.

NCAA Division III

- A coach can initiate a phone call at any time during PSA's High School career
    A PSA can initiate a phone call to any college coach at any time during their high school career.

Unofficial Visit

An unofficial visit is a meeting on campus where the prospective student-athlete visits the school at their own expense. A PSA can take as many unofficial visits as they like to any number of colleges at any time.

- The institution cannot provide any expenses including transportation, meals, or lodging.
- A prospective student-athlete can stay on campus but must pay the regular institutional rate for lodging.
- The institution may provide up to three complimentary tickets to an athletic event on campus
- A coach can provide transportation to an off-campus sporting event or athletic facility only if it is within 30 miles of campus.

Official Visit

An official visit is a formal campus visit by a PSA where the educational institution takes on the expense. The institution will pay all expenses or a portion of the expenses for the visit.

- In order for a PSA to take an Official Visit, the PSA must be registered with the NCAA Eligibility Center, and have taken the SAT/ACT, and submitted unofficial transcripts to the institution.
- Each PSA is allowed a maximum of five official visits
- Each PSA can only make one official visit to each institution
- An official visit can occur any time after the first day of the PSA's senior year.

Other details regarding official visits (optional)

- 48 hour maximum visit
- Commercial air transportation in coach class to and from airport
- A student-host is given $30 per day for entertainment
- A maximum of three meals per day during the visit
- Tickets to home athletic event for the PSA and their parents

Recruiting Chart 3 – 3 NCAA Recruiting Rules

	RECRUITING METHOD	MEN'S BASKETBALL	WOMEN'S BASKETBALL	FOOTBALL	OTHER SPORTS
SOPHOMORE YEAR	Recruiting Materials	• You may receive brochures for camps and questionnaires • You may begin receiving recruiting materials June 15 after your sophomore year	• You may receive brochures for camps and questionnaires	• You may receive brochures for camps and questionnaires	• You may receive brochures for camps and questionnaires • Men's Ice Hockey – you may begin receiving recruiting materials June 15 after your sophomore year.
	Telephone Calls	• None allowed	• None allowed	• None allowed	• None allowed
	Off-Campus Contact	• None allowed	• None allowed	• None allowed	• None allowed
	Official Visit	• None allowed	• None allowed	• None allowed	• None allowed
	Unofficial Visit	• You may make unlimited number of unofficial visits, except during a dead period	• You may make unlimited number of unofficial visits, except during a dead period	• You may make unlimited number of unofficial visits, except during a dead period	• You may make unlimited number of unofficial visits, except during a dead period

	RECRUITING METHOD	MEN'S BASKETBALL	WOMEN'S BASKETBALL	FOOTBALL	OTHER SPORTS
JUNIOR YEAR	Recruiting Materials	• Allowed • You may begin receiving recruiting materials June 15 after your sophomore year	• You may begin receiving September 1 of your junior year	• You may begin receiving September 1 of your junior year	• You may begin receiving September 1 of your junior year.
	Telephone Calls	• You may make phone calls to the coach at your expense	• You may make phone calls to the coach at your expense	• You may make phone calls to the coach at your expense	• You may make phone calls to the coach at your expense
	College coaches may call you	• Unlimited	• Unlimited September 1 of your junior year	• Once from April 15 to May 31 of your junior year	• Once per week starting September 1 of junior year.
	Off-Campus Contact	• Allowed beginning opening day of classes. Contacts other than April period may only occur at your school. Contacts in April may occur at your school o residence. • No contact on the day of a competition.	• Allowed September 1 at the beginning of your junior year • No contact on the day of competition	• None allowed	• Allowed starting July 1 after your junior year.
	Official Visit	• Allowed January 1 of your junior year	• Allowed April of your junior year beginning Thursday following the Final Four.	• None allowed	• None Allowed
	Unofficial Visit	• You may make unlimited number of unofficial visits, except during a dead period	• You may make unlimited number of unofficial visits, except during a dead period	• You may make unlimited number of unofficial visits, except during a dead period	• You may make unlimited number of unofficial visits, except during a dead period

	RECRUITING METHOD	MEN'S BASKETBALL	WOMEN'S BASKETBALL	FOOTBALL	OTHER SPORTS
SENIOR YEAR	Recruiting Materials	• Allowed	• Allowed	• Allowed	• Allowed
	Telephone Calls	• You may make phone calls to the coach at your expense	• You may make phone calls to the coach at your expense	• You may make phone calls to the coach at your expense	• You may make phone calls to the coach at your expense
	College coaches may call you	• Unlimited	• Unlimited	• Unlimited	• Unlimited
	Off-Campus Contact	• Allowed	• Allowed	• Allowed	• Allowed
	Official Visit	• You may make only one official visit per college and up to a maximum of five official visits to Division I colleges. There is no limit to official visits to DII colleges	• You may make only one official visit per college and up to a maximum of five official visits to Division I colleges. There is no limit to official visits to DII colleges	• Allowed beginning opening day of classes your senior year. • You may make only one official visit per college and up to a maximum of five official visits to Division I colleges. There is no limit to official visits to DII colleges.	• Allowed beginning opening day of classes your senior year. • You may make only one official visit per college and up to a maximum of five official visits to Division I colleges. There is no limit to official visits to DII colleges.
	Evaluations and Contacts	• Up to seven times during your senior year. • Unlimited number of contacts and evaluations the day after you sign an NLI, written offer of admission, and/or financial aid.	• Up to seven times during your senior year. • Unlimited number of contacts and evaluations the day after you sign an NLI, written offer of admission, and/or financial aid.	• Up to six times during your senior year. • Unlimited number of contacts and evaluations the day after you sign an NLI, written offer of admission, and/or financial aid.	• Up to seven times during your senior year. • Unlimited number of contacts and evaluations the day after you sign an NLI, written offer of admission, and/or financial aid.

RECRUITING METHOD	DIVISION II	DIVISION III
Recruiting materials	<ul><li>You may receive brochures for camps and questionnaires at any time.</li><li>A coach may begin sending you printed recruiting materials June 15 before your junior year.</li></ul>	<ul><li>You may receive printed materials any time.</li></ul>
Telephone calls	<ul><li>No limit on number of calls by a college coach beginning June 15 before your junior year.</li><li>You may make calls to the coach at your expense</li></ul>	<ul><li>No limit on the number of calls or when they can be made by a college coach</li><li>You may make calls to the coach at your expense</li></ul>
Off-campus contact	<ul><li>A college coach can have contact with you or your parents/legal guardians off the college's campus beginning June 15 before your junior year.</li><li>No limit on number of contacts off campus</li></ul>	<ul><li>A college coach may begin to have contact with you and your parents/legal guardian off the college's campus after your junior year.</li></ul>
Unofficial visits	<ul><li>You may make an unlimited number of unofficial visits any time, except during a dead period.</li></ul>	<ul><li>You may make an unlimited number of unofficial visits any time.</li></ul>
Official visits	<ul><li>You may make official visits starting the opening day of classes your senior year</li><li>You may make only one official visit per college; no limit to official visits to Division II colleges.</li></ul>	<ul><li>You may make official visits starting the opening day of classes your senior year</li><li>You may make only one official visit per college; no limit to official visits to Division III colleges.</li></ul>

New Legislation – NCAA Division I Effective Date August 1, 2014

In sport other than basketball, cross country/track and field, football, and swimming and diving, (1) to specify that telephone calls to an individual (or his or her parents or legal guardians) may be made at the institution's discretion beginning September 1 at the beginning of his or her junior year in high school; and (2) to permit any form of electronic correspondence (e.g., e-mail, instant messenger, fax, text messages) to be sent to a prospective student-athlete (or the prospective student-athlete's parents or legal guardians) as specified.

REVIEW IT!

1. When do I become a prospective student-athlete? _____

2. For your sport, when can a college coach call you for the first time?
   _____

3. For your sport, when can a college coach begin sending you recruiting materials?
   _____

4. How many unofficial visits are you allowed to take?
   _____

5. How many official visits are you allowed to take?
   _____

6. Can a college coach make a visit to your school to evaluate you during a practice and then meet with you following practice during your senior year?   **Yes**   **No**

7. You are a senior playing in a one day tournament where you will play two games. A college coach is allowed to come up to you following the first game to let you know that you played a good game and that they are interested in recruiting you. **True False**

8. Which of the following statements is TRUE concerning an OFFICIAL visit?

    A. An official visit may be made to an off-campus site 100 miles from campus if the institution is appearing in an athletics contest at that site.
    B. During the official visit a prospective student-athlete may receive complimentary tickets to a conference tournament.
    C. A Multi-sport prospective student-athlete may not receive more than 5 expenses paid visits, and not more than one per institution

Answers
1. 9TH grade 2. Varies 3. Varies 4. Unlimited 5. 5 6. Yes 7. False 8. C

CHAPTER 4 LEVEL OF COMPETITION

Which Division Should You Compete? There are differences between the DI, DII, DIII, NAIA, and NJCCA regarding athletic scholarships, athletic budgets, and playing seasons. In 2012 a total of 517,849 unique student athletes (i.e. multi-sport student athletes are counted only once) competed at the collegiate varsity level on teams sponsored by 2,058 schools. Unique student athlete participation by Athletic Association is as follows:

Recruiting Chart 4 – 1 Student-Athlete Participation Statistics

Athletic Association	Total # of schools	Total Athletes Participating	Men	Women
NCAA - Division I	348	139,063	77,323	61,740
NCAA - Division II	292	85,385	52,011	33,374
NCAA - Division III	418	144,062	86,370	57,332
NAIA	260	56,354	33,822	22,532
NJCCA - All Divisions	464	53,248	33,452	19,796
Other Associations & Independents	276	39,737	24,833	14,904
2012 Totals	2,058	517,849	308,171	209,678

There are many differences between Division I, II, and III Institutions. The myth is that the best players always play at Division I schools but that is not always the case. It is the prospective student-athletes college preferences which may determine the school they choose.

The Differences

Number of Programs

A *DI Institution* must offer seven sports for both men and women with a minimum of two team sports for each gender. Each gender must participate in all three sporting seasons sponsored by the NCAA.

A *DII Institution* must offer five sports for both men and women with a minimum of two team sports for each gender. Each gender must participate in all three sporting seasons sponsored by the NCAA.

A *DIII Institution* must offer five sports for both men and women with a minimum of two team sports for each gender. Each gender must participate in all three sporting seasons sponsored by the NCAA.

Athletic Scholarships (See Chapter 12 Financial Aid for Maximum Scholarship Amounts)

A *DI Institution* must meet minimum financial aid awards for their athletics programs. And each NCAA sponsored sport has a maximum number of scholarships it may offer.

A *DII Institution* has the ability to offer athletic scholarships. There are no minimums, it is the discretion of the university to determine how many scholarships will be offered for each sport. There are maximum number of scholarships that may be offered for each sport

A *DIII Institution* does not offer athletic scholarships. Many DIII programs offer Merit Scholarships which are academic and extracurricular activities combined.

Athletic Budgets; How Programs Are Funded

Division I: Split up into 3 segments based on football sponsorship.

- Football Bowl Subdivision – 125 schools
- Football Championship Subdivision (Formerly known as D-1AA) – 124 schools
- Non Football Schools - 98 Schools

The way a program is funded effects the following items for each program

- Coaching Staff
- Coaches Salary
- How a team travels
- College/University Apparel/Equipment
- Recruiting Budgets

The amount of funding put towards athletics for *Division II* and *Division III* institutions is at the discretion of each individual school. There are schools that are considered fully funded, and then there are schools who may only have part-time coaching staff. You need to do your research to find out how well funded each program is that you are interested in.

My Colleges by Division

Division I	Division II	Division III/NAIA
_____	_____	_____
_____	_____	_____
_____	_____	_____
_____	_____	_____
_____	_____	_____
_____	_____	_____

Playing and Practice Seasons

The Playing and Practice Season are broken into two segments for all divisions. There are certain time restrictions for each segment called Countable Athletic Related Activities (CARA) CARA activities include any **mandatory** team events (practice, conditioning, lifting, film, etc)

- Championship Season or Traditional Segment
- Non Championship Season or Non-Traditional Segment

Division I:

Championship Season

- 4 hours per day
- 20 hours per week
- 1 day off per week

Non-Championship Season

- 4 Hours per day
- 8 Hours per week
- 2 days off per week
- 2 hours per week can be skill instruction
- Number of Competitions varies by sport

In the Championship Season for Divisions I, II, and III all are allowed up to 20 hours per week of Countable Athletic Related Activities.

Division II:

Non-Championship Season

- 4 hours per day
- 8 hours per week
- 2 days off per week
- 1 day of competition

Division III

Non Championship Season

- Limited to 16 days of practice
- 1 Day of competition

The amount of time you must commit to your sport depends on the school and level of play you select. A student-athlete playing Division II or III will have much more down time than a student-athlete who plays Division I.

CHAPTER 5: PREPARING FOR THE SAT'S OR ACT'S

The three letters S.A.T usually frighten every high school student. The Scholastic Aptitude Test is made of three sections critical reading or verbal, math, and writing. It generally takes students approximately four hours to complete the exam.

You should make sure you are well prepared heading into the test. Every high school student should begin by creating a College Board account. Log onto www.collegeboard.org and sign up. The College Board website has a lot of uses like registering for the SAT's, taking practice tests, searching for colleges, and sending colleges your test scores.

As a student-athlete you need to make sure you send your test scores to each college you are interested in. In addition, you should send them to the NCAA Eligibility Center. **The code to send your test scores to the NCAA is 9999.**

THE SAT

The SAT measures developed verbal and mathematical reasoning abilities as they relate to successful performance in college. It is intended to supplement the secondary school record and other information about the student in assessing readiness for college. The SAT is made up of three sections.

- **Verbal Reasoning**
    - Analogies
    - Sentence completions
    - Critical reading passages
- **Mathematical Reasoning**
- **Writing**

THE ACT ASSESSMENT

The ACT Assessment is an alternative to the SAT, it is a standardized college entrance examination that measure knowledge and skills in English, mathematics, reading, and science reasoning, and the application of these skills to future academic tasks. The ACT Assessment consists of four multiple-choice tests.

- **English**
    - Punctuation
    - Grammar and usage
    - Sentence structure
    - Strategy
    - Organization
    - Style
- **Mathematics**
    - Pre-Algebra
    - Elementary Algebra
    - Intermediate Algebra
    - Geometry
    - Trigonometry
- **Reading**
    - Prose fiction
    - Humanities
    - Social Studies
    - Natural Sciences
- **Science Reasoning**
    - Biology
    - Physical science
    - Chemistry
    - Physics

Here are some other tips to help you battle the SAT's

- **Take the Test Early.** As a prospective student-athlete it is recommended to take your SAT's early. If you can afford it, consider taking the SAT's in the spring of your sophomore year, or early fall of your junior year as a practice test. Then you will know what subject areas you need improvement on. Many college coaches begin asking for SAT scores in the spring of their junior year. Having test scores allows coaches to get an idea if there will be any merit scholarships awarded.
- **Love books? You'll love the SAT.** The SAT directly tests vocabulary in its sentence-completion section. In order to excel, experts say students need to be well read and eager to look up words when they come across one they can't define in the years prior to the test.
- **Test Taking.** If taking tests has not been your forte through your academic life, the SAT might not be your best option. Testing experts say the test is best suited for students who don't mind being under the gun repeatedly and thrive under pressure. The test has nine sections, which means students must be prepared to answer questions in short bursts, something that could pose a problem for students who need to take time or skip around broader sections like those found on the ACT.
- **Don't get fooled.** While the math on the SAT is a bit easier than it is on the ACT, it's certainly not simple. Rather than relying on complicated concepts or delving into trigonometry, the SAT math section will oftentimes try to trick students who rush and don't read each question carefully, according to Carroll. He notes that the tricks aren't intricate, but they can be easily overlooked by students who aren't paying attention to detail. "The classic example is that [the test] often asks, 'What is X+1?' instead of 'What is X?'" he says. "And of course, the bad answer will be there. Your math and your calculations are perfect. X equals five and you circle five, but the answer is six."
- **When in doubt, leave it blank … sometimes.** One of the best-known strategies for tackling the SAT is to simply leave an answer blank if you don't know the answer. The test has a "guessing penalty" that punishes students who take a wild swing at a question that is beyond their intellectual reach by deducting points for incorrect answers. While leaving the answer blank on questions you don't know is a wise strategy, in some cases, it's actually better to guess. If you're able to narrow the answer down to two or three choices, guessing is the wiser option, as the odds of you getting the question right outweigh the penalty for a wrong answer. "I tell students, 'If you have no idea, skip it,'" says Carroll. "If you can narrow it down to two or three, you should be aggressive. Statistically, it will benefit you across the whole test."
- **Your mind may be ready, but prepare your body, too.** Nervous students oftentimes spend the weeks leading up to the test cooped up in their rooms, studying feverishly. Sometimes it's best to put the books down, get some fresh air, and clear your mind. Ahmad, who got a perfect score, runs cross country and claims that she garnered tremendous benefit by taking some time away from cramming and lacing up her running shoes. "One of the best things is to center the mind, get rid of that nervous energy, and clear everything out so that I had room

to absorb all of that information was to run," she says. "Staying active allowed my brain not to get overloaded because I had time to decompress."

- Plus, at roughly four to five hours, these tests require physical stamina. It's important to be rested on test day and let your body acclimate to the testing experience by taking timed practice tests. Just like training for a sporting event, your mind and body will be better prepared for the testing situation if you've been through it before.
- **Know the classes that matter.** On the math section, what you learned in algebra I and geometry comprise nearly everything on the test. It's most important to review those materials. There are some elements from algebra II, but they aren't tested heavily. The multiple-choice questions in the writing section test some of the basic elements of grammar, which regularly go uncovered in high school English classes. "If you've ever had a grammar class, that would help," says Carroll. "A lot of kids don't even know what a preposition is."
- **Use every second.** If you get bogged down trying to answer a question that has you stumped, skip it and revisit it using whatever extra time you have after you've worked through the full section. "You will do better on the test overall if you give each question its fair share of time, versus spending all your time on question number seven," says Alexis Avila, founder and president of Prepped & Polished, a Boston area-based college counseling and tutoring firm. "If you get stumped on any question, circle the question and go back to it at the end if time permits."

NEW CHANGES FOR SAT COMING IN 2016

Starting in the spring of 2016, some of the changes to the SAT will include:

- Instead of "SAT words" (depreciatory, membranous), the vocabulary words on the new exam will be ones commonly used in college courses such as "synthesis" and "empirical"
- The essay, required since 2005, will become optional. Those who choose to write an essay will be asked to read a passage and analyze how its author used evidence, reasoning and stylistic elements to build an argument.
- The guessing penalty, in which points are deducted for incorrect answers, will be eliminated.
- The overall scoring will return to the old 1600 scales, based on top of score 800 in reading and math. The essay will have a separate score.
- Math questions will focus on three areas; linear equations, complex equations or functions; and ratios, percentage and proportional reasoning. Calculators will be permitted on only part of the math section.
- Every exam will include, in the reading and writing section, source documents from a broad range of disciplines, including science and social studies, and on some questions, students will be asked to select the quote from the text that supports the answer they have chosen.
- Every exam will also include a reading passage from either one of the nation's "founding documents," such as the Declaration of Independence and the Bill of Rights, or from one of the important discussions of such texts, such as the Rev. Dr. Martin Luther King Jr's "Letter from a Birmingham Jail."

PHASE 2

COMMUNICATION
Build the Relationship

"COMMUNICATION IS THE BEST WAY TO CREATE STRONG RELATIONSHIPS"
- JADA PINKETT SMITH

OBJECTIVES

- CHAPTER 6 WHAT COLLEGE COACHES WANT
- CHAPTER 7 INITIATING CONTACT
- CHAPTER 8 INITIAL CAMPUS VISIT

CHAPTER 6 WHAT COLLEGE COACHES WANT?

Every college coach seeks something different in their recruits whether it be athletic, academic, or psychological attributes. These characteristics vary from coach to coach depending on the sport, the school, or the conference they compete in. The one thing you must understand is that a coaches' evaluation of a prospective student-athlete is subjective. It is not relevant what your coaches or parents say, it is up to the college coach to determine if you are the "right fit" for their program.

There are certain sports where statistics will tell the story of a prospective student-athlete's ability. In sports like golf, track, cross-country, rowing, and swimming the scores and times will determine if a prospective student-athlete can meet the athletic standards a coach is looking for. For many programs it's the academic and psychological attributes that coaches look at first. Coaches look for good students with a lot of character.

Every sport is different but it is helpful to get an idea of what coaches are looking for from the prospective student-athletes they recruit. The following coaches are well respected coaches within their sport and they are going to share their insights on recruiting and what they look for in prospective student-athletes.

- Sports camps are an excellent opportunity for an athlete to build skills, experience campus life, and connect with a coach. But athletes are usually not identified at camps. They are businesses that most often accept as many students that will pay to attend the camp, and the wide range of athletic ability makes them a bad place for coaches to recruit.
- Ask yourself these two questions when considering specific camps:
    o Has a coach from the school personally invited me to the camp?
    o Have I had any face to face contact with any of the coaches holding the camp?
    o If the answer to both of these questions is no, the only reason to attend the camp is to build skills or gain experience.
- If you do attend a college camp or clinic remember these things:
    o The other players attending are there for the same reason so you have to separate yourself from the crowd.
    o Upon your arrival, introduce yourself to the coaching staff.
    o Interact with the current players and ask them questions about the program
    o Follow-up after the event.

What College Coaches Say about Recruiting

In my years working in intercollegiate athletics I have built a network of college coaches and I asked some of them about their views on college recruiting. Here is what they had to say.

Jamion Christian, Mount St. Mary's University (D-I); Head Men's Basketball Coach

What is your Recruiting Philosophy?

We have a philosophy here that is built upon bringing in student athletes who are "peaking at the right time," both on the floor and in the classroom. We are in very competitive business in terms of looking for the best and the brightest and we have found that if we do intense research into each of our potential recruits that we can find those who have the best mental makeup to make an impact more immediately. Physically we want those who are younger in age this allows for the more likely chance to a growth spurt and their chances that we can maximize their potential while under our coaching. We are always looking to have a bigger stronger athlete for the longest duration of time within our program we can do this by being attractive to talented players who are a bit undersized but also younger than their competitors. Competitively we also want people who have shown that they value winning and who have done so playing the right way. Character mean's everything when you are projecting on how good someone will be down the road as a college senior those with strong character have a tendency to help improve a program in some way before they graduate. We want those who are passionate about being an important part of our program. When we are passionate about our university or our team we have a tendency to go the extra mile to make sure that we leave a lasting impression. Passion for achieving greatness makes your team and organization better.

How important is Academics in your recruiting?

The academic quality of the student athlete is extremely important. The recruiting process is a very difficult one because neither party truly understands what the other is completely looking for, the academic history of a student tells us a lot about how you operate on a day to day basis. Those who have a tendency to do well in class, have great relationships with the staff at school, and who have shown consistent improvement in the classroom most times will continue to do so at the collegiate level. That's not to say that if you struggled in something as a freshman that we won't recruit you but if you show improvement in those areas it shows us that you have a personality type that wants to be challenged and improve. We are looking for student athletes who are on the rise and who are fearless in their pursuit for perfection in all walks of their lives.

Qualities you look for in a PSA?

- Competitive
- Passionate
- Humble
- Productive
- Persistent
- Unconditional Buy in
- Unselfish
- Tough
- Appreciation
- Coachable

How important is the psychological/emotional attributes or character of a PSA?

Psychological and emotional toughness are extremely important when trying to evaluate potential student athletes. Seasons come and go quickly and because of that the pressure of the moment rises. Being able to handle the pressure and continue to be a productive team member will be the majority of a student athlete's experience. The sooner that a coach can understand the mental make-up of a player the sooner they will be able to coach them into becoming the best version of themselves as a person.

Advice to PSA about the recruiting process

> Go to the place where you are not only loved but wanted and needed. I've seen it to many times where student athletes choose a place that they do not want to go because of the level. Happiness cannot be measured if you have a burning desire to play. Choosing the wrong place may result in not playing and not fully enjoying your experience. Student athletes under estimate how much they want to play or the impact that they can make. Look at the depth chart: What year are the players at your position? Do they have any players currently like you on the roster? Does the teams style of play fit how you play best? If you write down five things that are extremely important for your happiness in college then stick to your personal game plan that you know will work for you.

5 things that are extremely important for my happiness in college

1. _____
2. _____
3. _____
4. _____
5. _____

Lindsey Munday, University of Southern California (D-I); Head Women's Lacrosse Coach

What is your Recruiting Philosophy?

My overall recruiting philosophy is finding student athletes that have a passion for the sport of lacrosse and for USC. There is an athletic component as well, and I look for potential for the student athlete to improve at the next level, but attitude and commitment are far more important than that to me. There are so many talented players out there, and I truly think the ones that succeed at the next level have the desire to improve, to work hard, and to fall in love with the process of becoming the best that they can be.

How important is Academics in your recruiting?

Academics are extremely important in recruiting. At USC, we need to present student athletes that will be successful academically. We do not have a set number of Student-Athlete's that we can get in. Admissions need to see that the Student-Athlete will work hard academically as well as athletically. In Lacrosse, you do not get paid to play professionally so it is my job as a Coach to set our players up for success outside of sports.

Qualities you look for in a PSA?

- Great Attitude
- Team First Player
- Gritty
- Athletic
- Intelligent
- Hardworking
- Never Satisfied
- Growth Mindset

How important is the psychological/emotional attributes or character of a PSA?

The psychological/emotional attributes of a Student-Athlete are extremely important and for me, carry much more weight than athleticism and skill. I truly think that a player's mindset is what makes them successful at the next level. It will not be easy and there will be hard times – what will a player do when their back is against the wall? Will they quit? Will they give up? Or will they buckle down and do whatever it takes to get better? Mindset is a skill and can be worked on and I look for that in PSA's.

Paul Royal, LaSalle University (D-I); Head Women's Soccer Coach

What is your Recruiting Philosophy?

We begin with the pure evaluation at National, Club and ODP events to identify the technical, tactical, physical and mental state of each player. Once this process is put into our database, we then rate those prospects among our immediate positional needs for that recruiting cycle. One of the main characteristics we look for is athletic thinkers that value the team before themselves. Once we've rated our elite recruits we do a tremendous amount of research on the character of that individual (What's their attitude like when things aren't going their way? What's their leadership role among their peers/teammates? What are their social habits like off the field? Do they value their relationships with their peers/teammates…and show respect to those individuals? Would they put the team before themselves? How do they handle stress and adversity? etc…). Each program has a different culture so we try very hard to find the person and player that fits our culture.

How important is Academics in your recruiting?

The most important area of concentration should be on their <u>academics</u>. If a player is academically sound their options are limitless academically, financially, and geographically when they go to choose a school. Our university's athletic department takes great pride in academic excellence as do each and every one of our players. It has to be the main reason why they are playing college soccer…to get a degree and provide a better life for themselves.

Qualities you look for in a PSA?

- High Integrity
- Selflessness
- Honest & Trusting
- Loyal
- Hardworking

- Passionate
- Committed to Excellence
- Invested in relationships
- Academic High Achiever

How important is the psychological/emotional attributes or character of a PSA?

For our program, we take great pride in having a strong mentality and "never quit" attitude. When we recruit individuals we take immediate notice during the recruiting process what type of mental and emotional stability they possess. We know that there will be a lot of ups and downs throughout their college career and life, so we are looking for someone that can deal with failure as well as deal with success.

Pat Horvath, Philadelphia University (D-II) Head Baseball Coach

What is your Recruiting Philosophy?

My overall recruiting philosophy is to find the best player to fit into the program. Will the player have success in school, will he be a positive representative of the baseball program on and off campus. Is he a team first player or an "I" first player. Does he know the game or is he just a showcase type of player. If he is a pitcher, does he throw strikes, what does the hitters look like when facing him. The school I am at I have to find pitchers that can pitch and keep hitters off balance I am not going to get the 90mph throwers. For hitters I am looking for guys that can consistently square balls up in a game.

How important is Academics in your recruiting?

Academics is important because that is the student-athletes main purpose for attending college. But for us the academic side is not as important in terms of our prospective student athletes to get accepted but rather the amount of financial aid they would receive. Academics is important for creating a better financial package. We are not a fully funded program so bringing in good students helps us bring in better recruits because we can offer them more financial aid by combining academic and athletic aid.

Qualities you look for in a PSA?

- Competitor
- Team Player
- Knowledge of the game
- Plays and Practices Hard
- Attention to Detail

How important is the psychological/emotional attributes or character of a PSA?

Psychological/emotional attributes are very important. They have to be able to deal with failure and the possibility of not playing all the time, which is new for some players. Some players will be able to handle that type of adversity and others will not. We want to find the players who will be able to handle that and use it as motivation to get better.

Advice to PSA about the recruiting process

First is to fill out any questionnaires that a coach sends you as soon as possible. Also to call a coach back if you missed their call. It shows them that you are interested or have at least the respect to call someone back. Another point would be to let a school know honestly if they are not a school you would consider or that you have decided to go somewhere else. Also make sure you fill out or turn in all paper work that is needed to the schools admission department, as well as sign up for the NCAA eligibility center.

Jessica Wolverton, McDaniel College (D-III); Head Women's Volleyball Coach

What is your Recruiting Philosophy?

My recruiting philosophy is to try and find the players who best fit into my current system who can compete at a high level. I might see a player who is very talented, but I don't think she can handle the toughness of my practices or the competitive atmosphere I have created so I do not recruit her. On the other side, there might be a player who fits great into my system but doesn't have the talent level to contribute on the court. This narrows the search process down quite a bit as to who I ask to be a part of my program. Each recruit has to have both characteristics I look for-a high level of ability and the willingness to adjust to my system in the gym.

How important is Academics in your recruiting?

I would say that academics is very important in recruiting. I work at McDaniel College, a high level private college with strict academic requirements for admission. If the player I am recruiting doesn't fit those academic requirements, I simply cannot recruit her. I always look for the best academic students I can find-and usually, they end up getting extremely large merit scholarships which helps me to yield them in this economic climate.

Qualities you look for in a PSA?

- Hard Work Ethic
- Mental Toughness
- Good Time Management Skills
- Has Priorities in order
- Personable
- Can follow instructions
- Can handle criticism
- Respectful of authority

How important is the psychological/emotional attributes or character of a PSA?

The psychological and emotional attributes and character of a prospective student-athlete are extremely important. One thing women's sports need to be successful is good team chemistry. I have never spoken to a coach of a woman's team who has said that they had poor team chemistry and that was not a factor in their performance. If I hear from any coach, teacher, recruiting coordinator that a recruit causes issues within the team or is not mentally tough in the gym, I immediately cross that recruit off of my list. In my program, all of the players are told to get along and respect each other or they won't be a part of the program. If I feel that they cannot handle that, I do not pursue them as recruits.

Jill Calloway, University of Maryland (D-I); Former Assistant Softball Coach

What is your Recruiting Philosophy?

Find the best well rounded athlete we can that fulfills as many of the qualities/standards we are looking for. The more we can see them the better. We like to follow them over several tournaments, games, and academic semesters as possible.

How important is Academics in your recruiting?

Super Important! If they don't have the work ethic and pride in their academics then it makes us question if they have the commitment to play at the highest level. They are a Student-Athlete, student 1st. We need to be able to get them in school before they can wear the jersey. And maintain good grades to continue to compete. Our goal is also to help young people get a quality education and our concern is for their academic success, as well as athletics success. We want to develop great people.

Qualities you look for in a PSA?

- Athletic
- Great work ethic
- Coach-ability
- Well rounded
- Healthy
- Respect for others
- Speed
- Extra-curricular activities
- Honesty
- Integrity
- Good Communication skills

How important is the psychological/emotional attributes or character of a PSA?

We need to have student athletes with the highest moral character and stable emotions.

Advice to PSA about the recruiting process

We are recruiting you, you need to recruit us as well. Do your research, only you know what the best fit is. Make the choice that is right for you, it's not about the money. And remember your goal is to get the best education you can.

Unconditional Buy In Dependability
Confidence
Responsible High Character Passion
Productive Persistent Gritty
Unselfish Competitive Athletic
Academic High Achiever
Personable
Hard Work Ethic Intelligence
Focus Never Satisfied Honest
Tough
Team Player Attention to Detail
Loyal Good Communicator Drive
Member of the Community Ambition
Speed
Coachable Committed Student
Growth Mindset
Invested in Relationships
High Integrity
Leadership Experience Tenacity
Committed to Excellence
Purpose
Versatility Good Time Management Skills
Respect of Authority Mental Toughness

Guiding Future Stars to Gaining Future Success

CHAPTER 7 INITIATING CONTACT

Now you have a list of 20-30 schools that you are interested in and you have a general understanding of the NCAA Recruiting Rules. It's time to begin initiating contact with the college coaching community. Maintaining regular communication with college coaches will be essential to your recruiting process.

Introduction Letter

When initiating contact with a college coach you should send a cover letter and student-athlete profile to the head coach introducing yourself and highlighting your academic and athletic achievements. Below is an overview of the introduction letter. The format for all of your correspondences with college coaches should always include three parts:

- **Purpose or Objective**: Why are you writing to the coach? State the intention of the letter. E.g. you are writing to express interest in the program, writing to set up a visit, writing to provide a tournament schedule, etc.
- **Value**: Who you are, what value could you bring to the program athletically, and academically. You should come see me play this weekend at ...... or I'm looking forward to attending your camp and being able to interact with you and your staff.
- **Follow Up**: The follow up needs to be clear, concise, to the point, and shows the coach you are serious about their program.

ORGANIZATION OF THE INTRODUCTION LETTER

Salutation	Address each letter personally – i.e. "Dear Coach Smith
Purpose	State the intention of the letter. You are interested in playing for their team. Be Specific!! Why are you interested in their program? Do your research!
Value	Describe yourself as student and as an athlete. Discuss your strengths, and your role on your team. Are you a team leader, captain, etc? Briefly describe honors, awards, you have received. Don't Brag!
Follow Up	Make a plan to follow up them regarding your teams' schedule, or setting up an unofficial visit. Request additional recruiting material like questionnaires, camp or clinic information.
Closing	Sincerely, All the best, etc. Make it your own
Signature	Your name

Student-Athlete Profile

The Student-Athlete profile is similar to a resume. It is a snapshot of who you are as a student and as an athlete. Coaches will not offer you an athletic scholarship strictly on your player profile just like a manager won't hire somebody strictly on their resume. The Student-Athlete profile will help you get a foot into the coaches' office.

ORGANIZATION OF THE STUDENT-ATHLETE PROFILE	
Objective	State your purpose
Academics	List Specific information like high school address, GPA, test scores, academic honors, and other extra-curricular activities.
Athletic Info	High School and club/AAU team info, coaches name, coaches contact info, individual achievements, and team honors.

Please see the sample profile

Student-Athlete Video

Creating a video will help you gain more exposure with college coaches. But a video alone will not get you recruited. By creating the right video it will allow you the opportunity to be able to get into a coaches office. Highlight videos are great but you need a video that will show a coach who you are as a student, an athlete, and as a person.

Tips on creating a recruiting video

- **Keep it Short!** A five-minute recruiting video is probably long enough to convey your skills. A highlight video is supposed to be like a movie trailer, it should show a coach your very best skills with no bells and whistles. First impressions are very important with coaches and most coaches can tell in the first 10 plays whether or not you are the type of recruit they are looking for.
- **Include a personal message** to go along with your highlights. If a coach has an opportunity to see you speak and talk about yourself and what you are looking for, it can go a long way.
- **Show a wide range of skills!** Use clips that show you're a well-rounded athlete. For example, if you're a basketball recruit don't just have highlights of you burying jump shots. Also include clips of you dribbling in transition, playing tough defense, or establishing good rebound position. While making sure that you have a wide range of skills coaches want to see.

CJ Smith 2015 # 9 FC United

1750 Sheffield Dr Blue Bell, PA 19422

(610) 277.7407   CJsmith9@gmail.com

Objective:

I am graduating in June of 2015 and I am interested in playing soccer in college at the Division I level where I will be challenged both academically and athletically. I would like to major in business or sport's management. I am looking for a small school that will give me a well rounded education. I am looking for a school where I will have the opportunity to play immediately.

Academics

High School: LaSalle High School   GPA: 3.2/4.0   Class Rank: 58/223
               16300 Cheltenham Pike
               Wyndmoor, PA 19161

Academic Honors: 2012 – 2014 Honor Roll (3.0 and above)

Test Scores: SAT: M 550   V 500   W 490   ACT NA

Extra-curricular: Member of the Ultimate Warrior Club (community service), SADD, Business Club

Athletic Info

Club Team: Fox Chase United (2008 – Present)   Position: Defender   Jersey # 9
Coach: Bill Zimmerman   Email: billzimmerman@gmail.com   Phone #: 215.825-6000

Team Honors/Awards: 2009-2013 EPYSA State Champions

   2013 - Jefferson Cup Premier Champions

Upcoming Tournaments: 2014 Jefferson Cup; Potomac Memorial Day Tournament

High School: LaSalle High School (2012 – 2013) Position: Defender # 9

Coach: Bob Johnson   Email: bobj2014@gmail.com Phone # : 215-872-1234

Team Honors/Awards: 2013 Philadelphia Catholic League Champions; 2013 District 1 Champions

Individual Honors: 2013 PCL 2nd Team Selection

   1 Goals and 3 Assists in 2013

Self-Assessment 7 – 1 Student-Athlete Profile

MY OBJECTIVE

_____
_____
_____

ACADEMICS

High School _____

Address _____

GPA (Grade Point Average) _____

STANDARIZED TEST SCORES	**HONORS/AP CLASSES**
SAT M_____ V_____ W_____	_____
ACT Assessment_____	_____

EXTRACURRICULAR ACTIVITIES

_____
_____

ATHLETICS

Height_____ Weight_____	Position_____
Club Team_____	High School_____
Club Coach_____	High School Coach_____
Email Address_____	Email Address_____

Team Awards/Accomplishments

_____	_____
_____	_____

Individual Awards/Accomplishments

_____	_____
_____	_____

Things you can include with your student-athlete profile

- Team schedule with dates and times
- Video
- Newspaper clippings about you and your team

Effective Communication Tips

When communicating with college coaches there is certain etiquette you should follow. Here are some tips when communicating with college coaches.

- Call, introduce yourself, and find out who you should contact before you start sending your information to a program. If you want to be considered, make sure they are expecting to hear from you.
- Include all of your basic information and correct contact information.
- Make sure you have professional email address. Consider creating a new one for recruiting purposes. Gmail is a good email provide because the use of Google Drive.
- If an athlete fails to respond to a coach, the coach might not think that athlete isn't interested in the program. To stay on a coaches' recruiting list, be prompt, thorough, and personal when responding to correspondence.
- Communicating with coaches is the single most important aspect of the recruiting process. It should come directly from the athlete, and it should come early.
- Reply to all correspondence you receive. Avoid judging universities based on name recognition. There are over 1,700 colleges at the NCAA Division I, II, III, NAIA, and Junior College levels. Don't ignore any of them.
- Provide coaches with regular updates about what's going on. Every three or four weeks.

Social Media Etiquette

- Make sure your voicemail, email, and Twitter handles are set up professionally, and are appropriate. These two small things make a huge difference in the recruiting process
- Think before you post or tweet. Pause for a second before you post or tweet and think about how your grandmother would feel about what you just said. Once you click it, there is no turning back
- Always remember that as a student athlete you not only represent yourself, but your school, coach, and teammates as well.
- Of course you would never violate any rules or laws, but in the unlikely event you do, don't share it with the world of Twitter or Facebook. There are hundreds of stories of careers ruined and scholarships lost over the stupidity of social media.
- Don't post daily about how hard you're working on the field/court/weight room/ etc. If you were really working that hard, you wouldn't have all the free time to tell us all about it.
- Avoid controversy. Politics, race, religion, and sexual orientation are generally a slippery slope.

CHAPTER 8 INITIAL CAMPUS VISIT

You have arrived on campus, took a campus tour, ate in the dining facilities, seen a typical dorm room, and walked through the academic building and now it is time to see the athletic facilities and meet with the coaching staff. You want to give a good first impression. You want to be confident, not arrogant, and genuinely interested in what the coach is saying about the school and their program. Your first official meeting with the coach is like a job interview. You want your personality and character to shine through in your first meeting with the coach.

Here are some of the most common questions you can expect to see from college coaches at any level, along with some tips on answering from a former college coach.

Whatever questions you are answering: sit up straight, look the coach in the eye, give a firm handshake, and speak politely, clearly, and confidently. These may seem like small things but you would be surprised on how much they can set you apart from the rest of the pack. A polished presentation can make all the difference in the world, especially to a coach who needs to gauge your character but doesn't have much time to do it.

- Connecting with the coaching staff before an unofficial visit is critical. The purpose of an unofficial visit is to experience campus life and build a relationship with the coaching staff. But if the coaches are not eager to host you, they likely are not interested in recruiting you.

- A student-athlete only has one chance to make a good first impression, so parents' help in building a child's confidence for communicating with adults is critical. Parents should start this process early so a coach does not mistake an athlete's shyness for lack of interest.

- Come prepared to "unofficial" visits; think of them as a preliminary job interview. If you're seeking a scholarship offer from a school, prepare some thoughtful questions about the direction of the program or about the school's academic reputation. This will show the coach you're interested and you did your research.

Self-Assessment 8 – 1 Personal Evaluation

1. **What are your strengths as a player?**
   Don't be modest. Don't Brag. "I have great ball control" or "I have good court awareness" is better than "I work hard."

   _____
   _____
   _____

2. **What are your weaknesses as a player?**
   Be honest, because the coach will know soon enough if you're not and that will reflect even worse on you than any weaknesses in your game. But keep it brief and don't sell yourself short.

   _____
   _____
   _____

3. **What improvements have you made recently?**
   This is a perfect follow-up to talking about your weaknesses.

   _____
   _____
   _____
   _____

4. **What kind of training regimen do you have?**
   Talk about any camps, weight training, or one-on-one coaching/training you've done. **BE HONEST!**

   _____
   _____
   _____

5. **What are your goals this season?**
   Aim high, but be realistic. Make sure you put plenty of focus on your team – you don't want to come off as a "me-first" athlete.

   _____
   _____
   _____

6. **What other schools are recruiting you? What other schools are you interested in?**
   If you're being recruited elsewhere, definitely tell them, but still make clear that their school is where you want to be.

   _____
   _____

7. **Why would you be a good fit for my school?**
   Make sure you've done your research – talk about the strength of their academics, especially in any programs that you are interested in. If their team has a particular history or reputation that you like, speak to that too.

8. **Do you think you are capable of playing at our level?**
   Absolutely you are – or you wouldn't be there. Explain how you can be an asset to their team.

9. **What type of scholarship are you looking for?**
   Always let the coach know if you have other offers on the table. Bring up financial issues if they will be a determining factor in your decision making. Be open to options and always ask about other types of aid besides athletic scholarship.

   _____
   _____
   _____

10. **How do you feel about playing time?**

11. **How do you feel about winning and losing?**

   _____
   _____
   _____

Guiding Future Stars to Gaining Future Success

12. **What are your interests outside of sports?**
13. **What can you offer me that someone else cannot?**

_____
_____
_____
_____

14. **Do you see yourself as a leader?** (Hopefully yes – if you honestly don't see yourself that way, explain how you're working on it!)

_____
_____
_____
_____

15. **What questions do you have for the coach?**

Always, always have questions prepared for the coach. It will show them that you are serious and spent time preparing beforehand. You may even want to bring notes. Please see Appendix V College Recruiting Organizer regarding every question a PSA should answer before committing to a school. But here is an opportunity to create some of your own questions. Here are some things to consider. Is there a pre-season? What is off-Season training like? Is there a travel squad? Is there academic support? What is your coaching philosophy? If you're prepared, polite, and confident, you will give a great first impression to any college coach you talk to.

1. _____
2. _____
3. _____
4. _____
5. _____

PHASE 3

GAINING EXPOSURE

Stand Out from the Crowd

GOOD, BETTER, BEST.
NEVER LET IT REST.
UNTIL YOUR GOOD IS BETTER,
AND YOUR BETTER IS BEST

- **TIM DUNCAN**

OBJECTIVES

- CHAPTER 9 GAINING EXPOSURE

- CHAPTER 10 NARROWING YOUR COLLEGE LIST

- CHAPTER 11 THE OVERNIGHT VISIT

CHAPTER 9 GAINING EXPOSURE

There are 3 key elements into gaining exposure in the college recruiting process

1. **Bring the Energy!**
2. **Get on the Radar!**
3. **Time to Shine!**

Bring the Energy

The first element in gaining college exposure is to bring energy and excitement into the process. Finding the right program can be a daunting task so you need to be energetic. You control your own athletic career and success relies on having a plan for success. What does bring the energy mean? Here are some tips:

Confidence

Be Confident! Having confidence in your athletic ability will feed the energy you put into your recruiting process. Athletes need to be confident in themselves to be able to reach their goals. "I will play collegiate athletics." "I will make the team."

Passion

College coaches love athletes who love their sport. Athletes who eat, sleep, and dream their sport will be successful because they are willing to work hard to be their best. Passion is what will keep your energy levels high.

Initiative

You are responsible for the path of the recruiting process. Just like taking the initiative on field or the court to get better you need to be proactive to get recruited. Self-starters are enthusiastic and bring loads of energy into every endeavor they take on.

Appreciation

You need to appreciate the opportunity you have been given. You need to appreciate the support you have been given over the years from your family, friends, teammates, and coaches. No matter what level you play at don't take anything for granted. You have worked hard to get where you are, and you have had a lot of support. Appreciate all of the good things in your life and who you are today.

Get on the Radar

Being energetic is only the first step to being recruited. You need to begin building relationships with college coaches. In the last chapter, we discussed initiating contact with college coaches which is the first step to building relationships with college coaches. The reason to build the relationship is to get on a college coaches radar so they have the opportunity to evaluate your athletic ability. Here are 4 ways that prospective student-athletes can effectively build relationships with college coaches throughout the recruiting process.

Email: Email is probably the most effective form of communication in the recruiting process. Coaches read, respond, and organize information about their recruits to help them gauge how interested a recruit is.

Phone: Phone calls are the quickest way to get interaction with a college coach. But there are strict rules for college coaches and phone calls. Please review the NCAA recruiting rules regarding phone calls pertaining to your sport. The responsibility of making a phone call is usually on the athletes. If you plan to call a college coach make sure you have a script prepared. The call should be short and to the point, about a 5 minute call will do the trick. Make sure you have at least 2 talking points, e.g. You are playing in a tournament this weekend and want to the coach to come see you play, or you are planning to come visit and wanted to see when the coach is available.

Text: Texting is the new thing in the world of communication. It can be an excellent tactic in the recruiting game as long as you don't overdo it. You should only text a coach after you have begun to develop a relationship with the coaching staff. If you have spoken to a coach on the phone or have met them in person it is ok to text them. But remember they are prohibited from texting you back. An occasional text can be a nice notification to a coach. Good texts are like tweets or Facebook status updates, simple and quick. If you are at a tournament and you know the coach is at the tournament a quick reminder that you are playing will go a long way. "Hey coach, my team is playing at 1 PM at field #3, hope you can make it." Or another one that will stick in a coaches head is a text after the coach wins a big game. "Congrats on the big win, good luck on Sunday."

Online Student-Athlete Profile/Website - An online presence is essential to your recruiting process. Recruiting folders are outdated, coaches are using mostly online programs to organize their recruiting. You need to have an online student-athlete profile to summarize and showcase who you are as a student and as an athlete. There are many recruiting service options out there for you to create a profile including BeRecruited, CSA, NCSA, NSR, and CaptainU just to name a few. However, coaches may not utilize them as much. Most coaches uses a Customer Relationship Management Tool like Front Rush. Front Rush allows coaches to store lists and contact data for every student-athlete that contacts them. Their Front Rush account is usually linked to a questionnaire that can be found on the programs website. It is essential that if you are interested in a program fill out their questionnaire immediately. This way you will gain access to their mailing list.

Time to Shine

You have done the work to get coaches to come evaluate you at a tournament, a camp, or clinic, now it is your time to shine. Going back to the first key element of gaining exposure, you need to bring the energy to the field or court. And that starts with having confidence walking on to the playing field. A coach will notice the way a player carries him or herself onto a field. Here are some tips for you to stand out among the crowd.

- **Be Confident!**
- **Be Positive!**
- **Be a Leader!**
- **Work Hard**
- **Play Hard**
- **Be respectful to your teammates, coaches, opponents, officials, and your parents.**

If you can do those things in addition to your athletic ability a coach will notice you. Coaches are not just looking for outstanding athletes, they are looking for extraordinary people, the total package as a student, an athlete, and as a person.

Athletically, coaches would like to see you play multiple times to have a good sense of your playing ability. Coaches don't want to judge you on one great performance or one terrible performance. So try not to get too high or too low on how you played in a game. A coach would like to find a players consistent performance. So they want to see you at your worst and at your best and at that point make a decision on you as a player.

How to Stand Out?

On the Field

> - Be the hardest working player on the field
> - Be vocal.
> - Be Encouraging
> - Control your emotions

Off the Field

> - Go out of your way to be recognized
> - Be Prompt
> - Be Respectful
> - College coaches will remember the little things. There are many players looking for the same opportunities you are so you have to separate yourself.

CHAPTER 10 NARROWING YOUR COLLEGE LIST

In order to start narrowing your list of colleges you need to ask yourself some questions. You should utilize some of the questions you answered when you began creating your initial list of colleges. You have created an initial list of 20-30 colleges but there is a good chance you and your parents will not have the time to visit over 20 schools so you need to begin narrowing down your list. Use the college recruiting organizer in Appendix V to begin managing the rest of your college recruiting process.

Self-Assessment 10 – 1 Narrow your College List

By thinking about and answering the questions below it should help you narrow your list to about 10-15 schools. You should really begin to delve deeper into each program by visiting campus and setting up a meeting with the college coach, if you have not already done so. You should also begin doing more research on each of the programs you are interested in. Things to consider:

General Recruiting Questions

Has your college preferences changed since you created your initial list of schools?   Yes   No

Have you selected colleges based on location or campus setting?   Yes   No

Is the size of the school a factor in your decision process?   Yes   No

Have you decided what level you would like to play?   Yes   No   Undecided

Is there a school or program where you haven't felt a real connection to?   Yes   No

Have you visited college campuses where you didn't feel comfortable or didn't feel like you could see yourself there?   Yes   No

Have you met or spoke to a college coach where you didn't feel like you would be a right fit for their program for one reason or another? Yes   No

Athletic Recruiting Questions

Do you like the coaching staff? How has your interaction been?

What is the coaches' philosophy, is it similar to what you are looking for?

How big is roster? How many at your position?

How many is the coach recruiting? How many at your position?

Is there opportunity to play right away?

What are the facilities like?

Table 10 – 1 My Updated College Lists Date: _____

	COLLEGE	DIV.	LOCATION	CONFERENCE	COACH	COACH EMAIL	COACH PHONE #
1.							
2.							
3.							
4.							
5.							
6.							
7.							
8.							
9.							
10.							
11.							
12.							
13.							
14.							

CHAPTER 11 THE OVERNIGHT VISIT

You have taken an initial visit to campus and liked what you have seen so far. It's time to delve in deeper and get a better feel for the campus and for the athletic program. You want to spend the night on campus for an unofficial or official visit depending on what year you are.

What are some tips for a PSA before they go on unofficial overnight or official visits?

The most ideal time to take an official visit is to take a Friday off from school and spend the day and night with players on the team. Meeting with the coaches and getting a tour of the athletic facilities is a good start but you want to spend time on campus with current players and the general student body.

- **Take a standard admissions tour** of campus (this enables you to see what other types of students are considering the school)
- **Go to classes** with a player on the team. Are classes what you expected? Can you see yourself in only small classes? Are large lecture halls suitable? While attending classes, notice the size of the class. Notice the ability of the professor. Would you feel comfortable learning in this situation? Don't be afraid to ask lots of questions. Ask about which classes are interesting or fun. Ask about how difficult it is to balance academics, athletics, and social life.
- **See where players eat meals**; you get a great idea of who they socialize with. Do they only eat with their teammates? Do they have friends outside the team? Are they in fraternities or sororities?
- **Go to a practice**; is there mandatory practice or conditioning? Are there captain's practices?
- Go out and see what a Friday night on campus is like? Are there lots of campus run activities? Do students go to campus parties? Do students go off campus?
- **Stay in underclassmen dorms** Do most students live on campus? Can you see yourself housing in a 2 person double or a 4 person suite? Are there coed dorms? Is campus housing close to the academic buildings?
- **Ask a lot of questions**. And just take in the experience and everything around you. Can you imagine yourself on campus going to classes, eating in the cafeteria, playing on those facilities? If you can say yes to those things, then that school might be the "right fit."
- **Remember it's a four year commitment** Most importantly make sure you are happy and you can see yourself living at the college for the next four years. Look around you and see if people are enjoying themselves.

PHASE 4

DECISION MAKING

Weighing your Options

"CHOOSE THE SCHOOL WHERE YOU ARE NOT ONLY LOVED BUT WANTED AND NEEDED"

- **JAMION CHRISTIAN**

OBJECTIVES

- CHAPTER 12 FINANCIAL AID
- CHAPTER 13 THE ADMISSIONS PROCESS
- CHAPTER 14 SELECTING THE RIGHT FIT
- CHAPTER 15 COMMITTING TO A SCHOOL

CHAPTER 12 FINANCIAL AID

The cost of tuition is a huge factor in choosing a college. Students do not want to graduate from college with tens of thousands of dollars in debt. Finding the right financial package is vital to the college selection process. There are number of different forms of financial aid that a student-athlete could receive.

- **Athletic Scholarship** – It is very rare in sports other than football and basketball that a student-athlete will receive full athletic scholarship. Approximately less than 1% of high school student-athletes will receive full grant in aid award. If you are awarded an athletic scholarship of any amount you will sign a National Letter of Intent, which we will cover later.

Athletic Scholarship Overview

The NCAA has set limits on maximum number of scholarships for each sport. There is no requirement by the institution to offer the maximum number of scholarships in that sport other than basketball and football. Here is a breakdown of Maximum Scholarships for the most popular NCAA Sports:

*The BCS Conferences (ACC, Big 10, Big 12, PAC 12, and the SEC) are permitted to offer multi-year athletic scholarships to prospective student-athletes. The smaller schools are still able to offer year to year scholarship offers.

Recruiting Chart 12 – 1 NCAA Maximum Scholarships for Men's Sports

Men's Varsity Sports	NCAA I	NCAA II	NAIA **	NJCAA **
Baseball	11.7	9	12	24
Basketball - NCAA I is a head count sport	13	10	-	15
Basketball - NAIA Division I	-	-	11	-
Basketball - NAIA Division II	-	-	6	-
Bowling	-	-	-	8
Cross Country - NCAA limits include Track & Field	12.6	12.6	5	10
Fencing	4.5	4.5	-	-
Football - NCAA I FBS - head count sport	85	-	-	-
Football - NCAA I FCS	63	-	-	-
Football - Other Divisions	-	36	24	85
Golf	4.5	3.6	5	8
Gymnastics	6.3	5.4	-	-
Ice Hockey	18	13.5	-	16
Lacrosse	12.6	10.8	-	20
Rifle - Includes women on co-ed teams	3.6	3.6	-	-

Skiing	6.3	6.3	-	-
Soccer	9.9	9	12	18
Swimming & Diving	9.9	8.1	8	15
Tennis	4.5	4.5	5	9
Track & Field - NCAA limits include Cross Country	12.6	12.6	12	20
Volleyball	4.5	4.5	-	-
Water Polo	4.5	4.5	-	-
Wrestling	9.9	9	8	16

Recruiting Chart 12 – 2 NCAA Maximum Scholarships for Women's Sports

Women's Varsity Sports	NCAA I	NCAA II	NAIA **	NJCAA **
Basketball - NCAA I is a head count sport	15	10	-	15
Basketball - NAIA Division I	-	-	11	-
Basketball - NAIA Division II	-	-	6	-
Bowling	5	5	-	8
Cross Country - NCAA limits include Track & Field	18	12.6	5	10
Fencing	5	4.5	-	-
Equestrian	15	15	-	-
Field Hockey	12	6.3	-	-
Golf	6	5.4	5	8
Gymnastics - NCAA I is a head count sport	12	6	-	-
Ice Hockey	18	18	-	-
Lacrosse	12	9.9	-	20
Rifle - Includes men on co-ed teams	3.6	3.6	-	-
Rowing	20	20	-	-
Rugby	12	12	-	-
Sand (Beach) Volleyball *	3	5	-	-
Skiing	7	6.3	-	-
Soccer	14	9.9	12	18
Softball	12	7.2	10	24
Swimming & Diving	14	8.1	8	15
Tennis - NCAA I is a head count sport	8	6	5	9
Track & Field - NCAA limits include Cross Country	18	12.6	12	20
Volleyball - NCAA I is a head count sport	12	8	8	14
Water Polo	8	8	-	-

Most NCAA varsity programs are <u>equivalency</u> sports which means awards can be split into partial scholarships in any proportion up to the maximum allowed. For example, an NCAA Division I school can allocate a number of partial athletic scholarships *equivalent* to 11.7 full scholarships in any amount among, say, 25 baseball players.

Full scholarships are relatively rare in equivalency sports. An additional caveat is that there is a top limit of the number of athletes that can be awarded even a partial scholarship in an equivalency sport - this limit is referred to as the maximum number of *counters*. For NCAA I baseball teams the maximum number of counters allowed is 27.

There are fewer NCAA head- count sports than equivalency sports; head count sports means the stated scholarship limit is absolute, and the number of student athletes receiving awards cannot exceed this number. NCAA I football and basketball are headcount sports as well as a few others noted above. For example, NCAA FBS football schools can have a maximum of 85 players under scholarship during a year. Head count sports generally award a much higher percentage of full scholarships to participants than equivalency sports.

All NAIA sports are equivalency sports for scholarship limits whereas all NJCAA sports are head-count sports for scholarship limits. For NAIA schools, aid to students who play at the junior varsity levels does *not* count in the overall limit on athletic scholarships.

NCAA & NJCAA Division III schools do not award athletic scholarships, but they do grant other forms of financial aid that student athletes may qualify for. Assistance to academically gifted student athletes can generally be exempted from counting as athletically based assistance only if the student athlete meets certain grade and/or test score criteria established by the various associations. Athletic scholarships are not awarded for participation in either club or intramural sports at any level.

The above numbers are *maximums* and schools can award less than the limit. Ivy League schools state they do not award scholarships based on athletic ability, but they grant other forms of financial aid as do many other schools. The US Military Academies (Army, Navy, and Air Force) do not award athletic scholarships, but all students receiving an appointment to the academies have their tuition paid in full.

The above limits are annual and apply to the entire team, so incoming student athletes at a four year institution are typically completing for approximately 25% of the maximum available scholarships.

If a sport is not listed, this indicates that it is not an official sport of the governing association and therefore is not subject to the scholarship limits. For example, Men's rugby is not an official sport of the NCAA and schools are not subject to NCAA athletic scholarship limits with respect to their Men's Rugby team. However, for many of these sports the respective teams have agreed to follow rules of other sport associations regarding scholarships and other assistance, often so a varsity level program does not receive a significant advantage over a competing club program from another school.

Other Forms of Financial Aid
- **Merit Scholarship** – Also known as an Academic Scholarship. Schools will award students financial aid based on their academic performance in high school which includes overall GPA and Test scores
- **Other Scholarships** -These are privately earned scholarships from your local community, companies, nonprofits, or churches. Any student-athlete is eligible to receive these types of scholarships since they can be based on intended major, academic achievement, ethnicity, or extracurricular activities. You should be aware any private scholarship based on athletic ability (i.e from your school's booster club, etc) could count against any Athletic Aid you receive."
- **Grants** – The most commonly known Grant is the Pell Grant. The Pell Grant is awarded to students based upon financial need. The grant is different than a loan, where as you do not need to repay the money back. Financial need is determined by the U.S. Department of Education using a standard formula, established by Congress, to evaluate the financial information reported on the *Free Application for Federal Student Aid* (FAFSA)
- **Work Study** - The FWS Program provides funds for part-time employment to help students in need to finance the costs of postsecondary education. Hourly wages must not be less than the federal minimum wage. Students must file a *Free Application for Federal Student Aid (FAFSA)* as part of the application process for FWS assistance.
- **Student Loans** – A student loan is a private loan with a bank that allows you to borrow money for college tuition but you must begin repaying that loan 6 months after you graduate.

- Once awarded a scholarship, a student-athlete must maintain it, which requires three things:
    - Performing well for the team
    - Adhering to the NCAA, NAIA, Conference, and School rules and regulations
    - Maintaining the required GPA
- Many of the best financial aid packages come from "non-scholarship" Division III programs. If a Division III program wants an athlete, it often finds a need- or non-need-based scholarship that applies to the student. Division III schools give financial aid based on how much they need a student-athlete, even if it is not in the form of "athletic" scholarships. You want to have multiple opportunities to negotiate the best scholarships possible
- DIII programs offer excellent opportunities that are often overlooked because DIII programs do not technically offer athletic scholarships. But DIII schools do offer grants-in-aid and non-athletic scholarships that can make the cost of attending less than DI & DII counterparts.
- College student-athletes earn, on average, between $12,850 (for in-state, public school students) to $21,266 per year (for private school students) in scholarships, grants, and financial aid every year. That adds up over the course of 4-5 years.

Table 12 – 1 My Costs of Colleges

Chart your course to see which college or university best fits your financial resources. Your totals in expenses and funds available should be the same amount. If you have a funding gap, meaning that you have more expenses than funds available then you will need to take out a loan (most likely), or vice versa (less likely). List Colleges in the top row

EXPENSES				
• Tuition and fees	$	$	$	$
• Room and board	$	$	$	$
• Books and supplies	$	$	$	$
• Transportation	$	$	$	$
• Miscellaneous	$	$	$	$
TOTAL	$	$	$	$
FUNDS AVAILABLE				
• Student and parent contribution	$	$	$	$
• Grants	$	$	$	$
• Athletic scholarship	$	$	$	$
• Merit scholarship	$	$	$	$
• Private scholarship	$	$	$	$
• Work Study	$	$	$	$
TOTAL	$	$	$	$
Funding Gap	$	$	$	$

CHAPTER 13 THE ADMISSIONS PROCESS

You are a senior who may have already verbally committed to a school or you are still deciding between a few options. It's time to start the Admissions Process. College applications and college essays can be stressful for any high school student.

COLLEGE APPLICATIONS

A college application is part of the competitive college admissions system. Admissions departments usually require students to complete an application for admission that generally consists of academic records, personal essays (as well as samples of high school work), letters of recommendation, and a list of extracurricular activities such as club membership and volunteer work. Some schools require the SAT or ACT, while others make it optional. Deadlines for admission applications are established and published by each college or university.

- Many coaches and admissions departments coordinate their recruiting efforts. Coaches will often check transcripts with the admission's counselor responsible for athletics to see if a student-athlete is admissible.

- It is important to get to know your admissions counselor, as well as the coach, so both departments know you as a student and an athlete.

- Take advantage of admission visit days so you can experience all aspects of the college or university. Admitted Student Days, for example, may allow you to meet professors in your major, or meet students outside of athletics which can help you make an overall decision on a school's fit."

- It's important to understand the different types of Application Deadlines
    - **EARLY DECISION :**
      Early Decision (ED) is a method of application that you can use for only one college; if you consider applying ED, it must be your absolute first choice dream college. ED applications are contractually binding, and stipulate that if you are accepted, you will (read: MUST) attend that college or university. It's a great way of getting your application in earlier.

    - **EARLY ACTION**:
      Applying Early Action gives you the benefit of receiving an early admission decision, just as with Early Decision, but it is non-binding, and you can often apply Early Action to more than one school. Early Action deadlines are generally the same as Early Decision deadlines, with the exception of sending in a deposit: that deadline is usually the same as the Regular Decision deadline.

- **REGULAR**

    This is the most common type of application, and the type that people know most about. Applying Regular Decision involves sending out your applications typically around the beginning of January, and you can apply to as many schools as you choose. Admissions decisions are sent out around the middle to the end of March, and deposits are usually due on May 1st.

- **ROLLING**

    Rolling admission is not a form of application, but a way that many schools release their admissions decisions. Instead of releasing admissions decisions on one day, colleges that use a rolling system send out admissions decisions when they are made, on an applicant-by-applicant basis. Rolling admissions is a system used only with Regular Decision applications.

Tips for creating your best college essay

- Think about who you are, strengths and weaknesses, values and beliefs.
- Create an outline or notes from the essay prompt
- Just start writing to get your thoughts down on paper.
- Organize Essay into three sections
    - Introduction/Thesis – One Paragraph
    - Body – Several Paragraphs
    - Conclusion – One Paragraph
- Find your focus – Be Specific
- Be creative
- Be Honest
- Receive Feedback
- Proofread and make corrections
    - Let your writing reflect who you are. An admission counselor wants to get to know you through the essay.
    - Fully answer the essay prompt chosen from the application

COLLEGE ESSAYS

The college essay is a vital part to your college application because it reveals your personality and character that your grades and test scores do not. It will give the admission counselors a sense of who you are as well as show off your writing skills.

College essays show how you think and how you write. They also reveal additional information about you that is not on other application materials. Not all colleges require essays, and those that do often have a preferred topic.

Table 13 – 1 My College Applications

Keep track of your applications by inserting a check mark or the completion date in the appropriate column and row. Write the Schools you are applying to in the top row.

School					
Unofficial Visit					
Campus Interview					
Official Visit					
Letter of recommendation					
(1) NAME					
Date Requested					
Follow-Up					
(2) NAME					
Date Requested					
Follow-Up					
Test scores requested					
Transcripts sent					
Application completed					
Essay completed					
All signatures collected					
Financial Aid forms enclosed					
Application fee enclosed					
Copies for all documents					
Letters of Acceptance					
Colleges notified of intent					
Tuition deposit sent					
Housing and other forms sent					
Orientation scheduled					

CHAPTER 14 SELECTING THE RIGHT FIT

Utilizing the tools provided in Chapter 10: Narrowing your list, you should have cut your list down to 4 or 5 schools. It's time to compare schools using your top criteria. You should sit down with your parents to discuss your options. When making your final decision there are many things to consider.

Factors to consider when choosing between colleges.

- **Type of School**
- **Size**
- **Setting**
- **Location**
- **Athletics Program**

- **Academic Programs**
- **Academic Environment**
- **Financial Aid**
- **Retention rate**
- **Graduation Rates**

- PSA's should pick a school where you will best be able to develop academically, athletically, and personally. If you can find a school that allows you to develop in those three aspects of your life then you have found the "RIGHT FIT"
- Don't always choose the program that gives you the best financial package it might not be the "RIGHT FIT"
- Choose a school that you will enjoy if you weren't playing a sport. You never know what could happen. It's important to pick a school, not just an athletic program. If you were unable to play your sport anymore would you be able to stay at the school and finish your degree?

GFS WANTS YOUR FEEDBACK

@GuidFutureStars

#CollegeRecruitingPlaybook

Table 14 – 1 College Comparison

Fill in your top 10 selection factors in selecting a college. Once you have you narrowed your search to five colleges, fill in the schools across the top row. Using a scale of 1 to 5, where 1 is poor and 5 is excellent, rate each college by your criteria. Total each column to see which college rates the highest based upon your criteria.

SELECTION CRITERIA					
1.					
2.					
3.					
4.					
5.					
OTHER CRITERIA					
6.					
7.					
8.					
9.					
10					
TOTAL					

Refer back to Self-Assessment 1-1 where you rated the factors that are most important to you in your college search.

Type of College　　_____　　　　Size/Enrollment　　_____

Geographical Location　_____　　Level of competition　_____

Campus Setting　　_____　　　　The Athletic Program　_____

Cost　　　　　　　_____　　　　Academic Standards　_____

Learning Environment　_____　　Graduation Rates　　_____

CHAPTER 15 COMMITTING TO A SCHOOL

The speed of NCAA recruiting has increased over the last decade. PSA's have been known to verbally commit as early as their sophomore year in high school.

Verbal Commitment

The NCAA defines a verbal commitment as a college bound student-athlete's commitment to a school before he or she signs a National Letter of Intent. The PSA can announce a verbal commitment at any time. This commitment is not binding for either the school or the PSA. Only signing an NLI accompanied by a financial aid agreement is binding by both parties. It is general rules among the NCAA community that verbal commitments belong to the coach not the institution. So, if a coach was to lose his job or take a new job there is no guarantee the new coach will keep that commitment.

Before you decide to verbally commit to a school you should make sure you are a million percent sure this is where you want to attend college.

Signing Day

The day has come when all of your hard work, sacrifices, commitment, and dedication on and off the field has paid off. You are receiving an athletic scholarship and you are signing a National Letter of Intent to play your sport at a Division I or Division II institution. Every kid dreams of the day they are at their school in front of their friends and family to sign their NLI that says I am receiving an athletic scholarship to play in college.

Million Percent Rule

As a former college coach, our program wanted to make sure when we received an early commitment that we had a strong verbal commitment from the prospective student-athlete. We used the million percent rule. Everybody involved including the PSA, the parents, and the coaching staff were a "million percent" sure that their school and program was the right fit.

National Letter of Intent

The NLI is a binding agreement between a prospective student-athlete and an NLI member institution

- A prospective student-athlete agrees to attend the institution full-time for one academic year (two semesters or three quarters).
- The institution agrees to provide athletics financial aid for one academic year (two semesters or three quarters).
- Basic penalty for not fulfilling the NLI Agreement
    - A student-athlete has to serve one year in residence (full time, two semesters, or three quarters) at the next NLI member institution and lose one season of competition in all sports.

Walking – On

There are other avenues besides signing an NLI to play intercollegiate athletics. There is the opportunity to be a walk-on. There are two types of walk-ons, a recruited walk-on also known as a Non-Scholarship player and a regular walk-on.

Recruited Walk-On

A recruited walk-on or non-scholarship player is a commonly used term to describe an athlete who is recruited by a college coach but is not offered an athletics scholarship for freshmen year. These athletes typically have a lot of interaction with the coaching staff and are usually offered a roster spot at the beginning of the season.

Regular Walk-On

A regular walk-on is used to describe an athlete who is not typically recruited by a college coach. The student-athlete intends to attend a school and then decides they would like to play in college. The regular walk-on must attend tryouts in the beginning of the season. Some program don't offer regular walk-on opportunities until their off-season.

What questions should you ask coaches if you are considering walking-on?
- Am I a recruited walk-on?

- How many walk-ons do you plan on taking this year?

- Do your walk-ons actually see playing time?

- Will you guarantee that I will earn a roster spot?

- Is there potential for me to earn a scholarship in the future? If so, what will this be based on and can you put it in writing? (Having this in writing is good, but it still lacks the binding nature of an NLI – it's just the coach's word)

- Will I have access to the academic support systems available for scholarship athletes, such as tutors, preferential course registration etc.?

- Will I receive the same equipment, clothing and access to the training table as scholarship athletes?
- Do I report to campus at the same time as the scholarship athletes?

DID YOU COMMITT TO A SCHOOL? GFS WANTS TO KNOW! TWEET @GUIDFUTURESTARS USING #GFSCOMMITTED AND TELL US WHERE?

My Recruiting Game Plan

1. **CONTINUE TO IMPROVE ACADEMICALLY AND ATHLETICALLY**
    a. ACADEMICALLY – Increase your GPA, take SAT/ACT, and takes the right classes
    b. ATHLETICALLY - The physical demands of playing college sport is much greater than in high school so continue develop physically, tactically, and your knowledge of your sport.
2. **BUILD A LIST OF 20-30 COLLEGES THAT YOU ARE INTERESTED IN AND FIT YOUR ACADEMIC, ATHLETIC, AND PERSONAL NEEDS**
    Create a balanced list of NCAA Division I, II, and III schools. Be open to all opportunities. Be Realistic.
3. **BUILD A CUSTOMIZED MARKETING PLAN**
    Create a quality student-athlete profile. It is important to have key academic data, athletic data, photos, video footage, etc, ready and available to provide to each coach. Write a sample introduction letter to college coaches to model but tailor each letter to fit the school, program, and coach you are sending it to. No Form Letters!
4. **REGISTER WITH THE NCAA ELIGIBILITY CENTER**
    If you are serious about playing at the NCAA Div. I or NCAA Div. II level you should register with the Eligibility Center by the start of your junior year.
5. **CONTACT COLLEGE COACHES**
    College coaches will not discover you magically. Take the initiative and contact coaches directly through email and phone. A phone call is much more powerful than an email. Maintain constant contact with coaches to build the relationship.
6. **VISIT COLLEGE CAMPUS'**
    College coaches will take you more seriously if you visit their campus. Campus visits allow you to get a real feel for the school. And ask yourself can I see myself here for the next four years of my life?
7. **NARROW YOUR COLLEGE CHOICES TO TOP 10**
    After doing your research and communicating with coaches begin narrowing your lists. Increase conversations with coaches about scholarship opportunities.
8. **REQUEST AN OVERNIGHT VISIT**
    The most telling of the recruiting process is spending the night on campus. You have the opportunity to interact with current players, watch a practice, attend a class, etc. You have the chance to live a day in the life of student-athlete at that school.
9. **MAKE A DECISION**
    Weigh all your options, speak with your parents, but ultimately choose the school where you will flourish.

PHASE 5

BEYOND THE DECISION
What's Next?

"SUCCESS IS NO ACCIDENT, IT IS HARD WORK, PERSEVERANCE, LEARNING, STUDYING, SACRAFICE, AND MOST OF ALL, LOVE OF WHAT YOU ARE DOING OR LEARNING TO DO."

- *PELE*

OBJECTIVES

- CHAPTER 16 ACADEMIC PREPARATIONS
- CHAPTER 17 ATHLETIC PREPARATIONS

CHAPTER 16 ACADEMIC PREPARATION

Congratulations! You have made your college decision, now what? Picking a college is a sense of relief for most high school students. For high school student-athletes, however, the work has just begun. Once you have made your college decision there are many factors to consider. The time frame when a student-athlete commits to stepping on campus for the first time as a college student varies for each individual. Some may commit in their junior year, or some may make the decision in the spring of their senior year. Depending on when you commit your plan of action will be different. The question you need to ask yourself is, "what do I need to do to be ready for the 1st day of classes?" Whether that is 18 months away or 3 months away, the answer will guide you through your plan of action. There are a number of items you must complete before you arrive on campus for the first time as a college student.

Post High School Check List

- **Complete NCAA Eligibility Center Paper work**
  - Follow up with your high school guidance counselor to make sure official transcripts are sent to the NCAA Eligibility Center.
  - Complete the Amateur Certification on the Eligibility Center website
  - Follow and Track your status on the Eligibility Center website
  - www.eligibilitycenter.org
- **Complete all paperwork necessary prior to arriving on campus**
  - Completed Medical forms and insurance documents
  - Financial Aid, Scholarship, and Loan information

The transition from high school to college for any student is a big jump but for a college student-athlete, there are added responsibilities. In order to be a successful college student-athlete you need to know how to balance everything in your life from school work to athletics, to maintaining friendships. This is no easy task. The most important aspect to be successful in college is time management. You need to be able to prioritize the things in your life. And for a college student-athlete the order is Academics, Athletics, and everything else. The "everything" else is up to you but those first two cannot change. The summer prior to your first semester you should begin creating daily and weekly schedules, to do lists, etc. to begin preparing for life as a college student-athlete.

Student-Athlete Success Playbook, an essential guide for any college freshmen student-athlete, it will assist student-athletes in helping them balance life as a college student-athlete.

Student-Athlete Success Playbook coming in 2016!

http://www.guidingfuturestars.com/Student-Athlete-Success.html

CHAPTER 17 ATHLETIC PREPARATION

One of the hardest adjustments to make from being a high school student-athlete to a collegiate student-athlete is the physical demands of college athletics. It is important for high school student-athletes to prepare themselves for the next level. The majority of college programs provide their athletes a summer workout but the earlier you can start working out the better. Organized lifting workouts and supervised running sessions should begin during the summer. Specific running times and days will be given by your new strength and conditioning coach or your specific team coach. Maximum fitness levels can be generated by the start of your training camp if you sustain disciplined work habits throughout the entire off-season.

The end of your season to the start of the following season.

Do not become inactive during this period. Schedule a vacation early to recover mentally and physically from the demands of your season or training sessions and then resume your training. You should report to school in peak condition. This is most important for a freshman entering into their first year. If you come into to the school year in sub maximal shape it will look bad for you and could potentially affect how you're playing time is viewed going into the start of the fall or spring seasons.

In order to play your best you have to practice good solid habits throughout the year. Here are some guidelines:

1. Players remain disciplined on and off the field.
2. Sound nutrition habits and adequate rest are crucial.
3. Players exhibit near maximum effort each weight workout.
4. Practice fast and play fast to develop fitness levels needed to play the game.

The fitness formula for a well-conditioned athlete is a simple one. There are no shortcuts, no magic pills or potions. A long-term commitment is necessary to reach and maintain your full physical potential. Many athletes can be disciplined for a workout, a week, or a month. The commitment of a true athlete is for his entire career.

> As a PSA who is prepared to enter their freshmen year you may be given an off-season workout packet. You are prohibited from receiving that from the coaching staff until after you have graduated from high school.

Do not kid yourself and think that you can get into peak physical shape in the two weeks leading into the season. A solid fitness level can be gained and utilized over a strenuous 8 week training period. The best athletes are the ones that stay active and healthy during the off season. Take advantage of the time that you have and plan to come into the start of your career in peak physical shape.

APPENDIX

GREATNESS, IS A LOT OF SMALL THINGS DONE WELL
- ***RAY LEWIS***

I.	COLLEGE RECRUITING TIMELINE
II.	GOAL SETTING
III.	TIME MANAGEMENT
IV.	WEIGHTED PROS CONS LIST
V.	COLLEGE RECRUITING ORGANIZER

APPENDIX I College Recruiting Timeline

Freshmen Year – 9th Grade

- Build strong academic, language, mathematics and critical thinking skills by taking challenging courses.

- Study hard and get excellent grades. Use the various school resources available at your school if you are struggling with certain classes.

- You can't use the excuse I don't have the time…build study time into your daily schedule. If you are on a block schedule do you're A Day homework on the A day and of course B Day homework on B days. Putting off homework creates poor study and preparation habits. Be diligent and stay on top of the work. Also don't study for tests the night before the test. Review material over the period of several days. Rewrite your notes on the subject. Research has shown that an individual will retain more information by re-writing ones notes or study guide material versus just reading over the material trying to memorize the information.

- Meet your guidance counselor and create a four year plan.

- Browse through college literature or surf the Web to get an idea of what kinds of schools may be of interest to you.

- Keep an academic and extracurricular portfolio.

- Take the PSAT. Look over the results of the tests to see the areas that need to be strengthened. At this time the math sections may be above grade level however the English area will provide an accurate assessment of vocabulary, sentence structure and reading comprehension.

- Know the NCAA academic eligibility requirements if you want to play sports in college. 16 core classes required for graduation.

- Participate on high school athletic teams.

- Begin to create a Student Player Profile/resume to send to college coaches: include academic and athletic accomplishments.

- At the end of the year met with your high school counselor to review your freshman year performance and results. Make any adjustments in your schedule to stay on track to graduate.

Summer Ideas:

- Look for summer employment opportunities like lawn care, child care, lifeguarding, and camps.

- Look for volunteer positions. Local community programs sponsored by churches, hospital, nursing homes etc. These experiences can prove invaluable on a college application.

- Attend summer college camp where several college coaches will be in attendance. Many college camps have just the respective college coaching staff or its players working the camp.

Sophomore Year - 10th Grade

• Begin to think seriously about the college admissions process.

• Continue to focus on achieving academic success. Make an appointment with your guidance counselor so that you can discuss your plans for high school and college.

• Attend various college fairs and visit colleges.

• Participate on high school athletic teams

• Keep record of all academic and athletic achievements and statistics as well as update your resume

• Participate in a volunteer/service activity and other extracurricular activities both at school and in the community. A depth of involvement is important.

• Take the PSAT. Use the results to evaluate areas that you need to strengthen in the math or English areas.

• If possible over breaks in school calendar or in the summer visit college campus and take their admissions tours to gain insight to the type of school settings that may interest you.

• Seek out leadership opportunities and make good decisions with your friends and classmates both in and out of the classroom.

• Build positive relationships with your teachers, coaches, guidance counselor and even your school administrators. They can provide invaluable insights to what you may do upon graduation. Also they can provide key recommendations for your college application.

Summer Suggestions:

• Again look for employments similar to your freshman year and summer camps with colleges that may be of interest.

• Begin to contact college coaches via their respective college website. Be realistic with the colleges you are considering in terms of your playing abilities. Look for those schools that fit your long term goals academically first. Don't choose the college program strictly for the coach. Create a list of at 15-20 colleges. Shoot for the stars on a couple of schools based on your academic profile; then 3-4 school in the middle and then 3-4 "safety" schools. You will be surprised to the number of students who only apply to 2-3 schools only who are not admitted and do not have a college to attend upon graduation.

Junior Year - 11th Grade

- Register for the NCAA Clearinghouse. All student-athletes must register with the clearinghouse to participate in NCAA Div. I or II sports programs. Submit transcript requests to the Guidance Office as soon as you register.

- Research exactly what you are looking for in a college. Think about: location, student body, academic requirements, size, academic structure, workable majors, campus life & cost.

- Narrow your list to 10-15 colleges that you may consider. During the summer or into the fall of your junior year contact the respective college programs alerting them to the tournaments or camps you may be attending.

- **DO NOT WRITE TO INQUIRE ABOUT ATHLETIC SCHOLARSHIPS!!!!! THAT IS A MAJOR RED FLAG AND A REAL TURNOFF TO THE COLLEGE COACHING STAFF**

- Taking competitive classes not just the basic elective classes are important. Only the GPA in the core classes will be counted for NCAA eligibility purposes. Non-core electives like Gourmet foods will not be factored into your NCAA core eligibility GPA.

- Take the SAT's or ACT's twice if possible. Colleges will accept both tests. Check out both test and see which one suits the testing abilities of your son or daughter. Your guidance counselor will be able to discuss the differences between the two tests.

- If the individual who is self-motivated and is looking for some ACT or SAT fine tuning preparation the following options could be viable:

    o Books from a bookstore or library on SAT and ACT preparation

    o Internet: Check out the College Board website at www.collegeboard.com they have the question of the "SAT Question of The DAY"

    o Some high school have a SAT prep class that may be helpful but the student has to be motivated to work

- Assess your grade point average with your SAT scores to the NCAA qualifier index to determine eligibility status. Need to have a certain GPA as well as SAT score to be a qualifier for NCAA Division I and NCAA II programs which allows you to play in your freshman year in college.

- Watch where seniors go. Talk to them about their choices.

- Ask your coach for a realistic athletic evaluation. Which college should you target?

- Visit the Career Center in your high school for assistance with SAT/ACT registration and test preparation, college reference materials (i.e., virtual tours, catalogs, applications, etc.), career resource catalogs and books, financial aid and scholarship reference materials and offerings, summer enrichment programs, and local student job opportunities.

Senior Year - 12th Grade

FALL

• Make decisions! Which colleges are you applying too?

• Write college essays (check college websites for essay requirements).

• Submit Secondary School Report form from your college application(s) and Transcript Release forms to your guidance counselor for each college you are applying.

• Make arrangements for final visits to colleges, if necessary.

• If you have not secured a place to play in college look to correspond with programs like Division II, Division III, NAIA or even junior colleges. Many are still looking to complete their recruiting classes. You can still seek out playing opportunities though they may be limited through the spring term.

• Search for and complete scholarship applications.

• Notify your guidance counselor when you receive any acceptances

WINTER

• Get financial aid forms: Federal Application Free Student Aid

> o (FAFSA) which is required by all colleges (available in December) if you want to be eligible for financial aid. Parents should complete the FAFSA as soon as possible, but not before January 1. The student will need to register for a PIN number as well as the parent/guardian. You will need your tax returns for both the student and the parent/guardian to complete the FAFSA form. Do this no later than March 15. Money is on a first come first serve basis.

• Do not delay in waiting to apply for Financial Aid. Financial Aid monies are becoming very tight at the private institutions throughout the country by the beginning of March especially with the rolling admissions colleges. If you delay you may miss out on an aid package.

• Midyear grades will automatically be sent to all colleges and universities to which you have applied.

SPRING

• As your decision letters arrive, inform your counselor and continue to think about your options.

• Complete housing and health forms.

• BE REALISTIC…your second choice school may be your first choice!

• APRIL 15th: The date all colleges will let you know their decision.

• MAY 1st: Candidates Reply Date – The date by which you MUST let colleges know your decision. Also, the date by which a deposit must be made at the college you will attend.

APPENDIX II GOAL SETTING

Setting goals and planning can be the difference between success and failure. Goal setting and planning go hand and hand. When you set goals, you need to create a plan to reach them. You should make short-term goals and long-term goals. The goals that you set should be S.M.A.R.T goals.

- **Specific** - Goals should be simplistically written and clearly define what you are going to do.
- **Measurable** - Goals should be measurable so that you have tangible evidence that you have accomplished the goal. Usually, the entire goal statement is a measure for the project, but there are usually several short-term or smaller measurements built into the goal.
- **Achievable** - Goals should be achievable; they should stretch you slightly so you feel challenged, but defined well enough so that you can achieve them. You must possess the appropriate knowledge, skills, and abilities needed to achieve the goal.
- **Realistic** - Goals should measure outcomes, not activities. A goal must represent an objective toward which you are both *willing* and *able* to work. A goal can be both high and realistic; you are the only one who can decide just how high your goal should be. But be sure that every goal represents substantial progress.
- **Timely** - A goal should be grounded within a time frame. With no time frame tied to it there's no sense of urgency. Your goal is probably realistic if you truly *believe* that it can be accomplished. Additional ways to know if your goal is realistic is to determine if you have accomplished anything similar in the past or ask yourself what conditions would have to exist to accomplish this goal.
- **My goal is** _____

SPECIFIC	
MEASURABLE	
ACHIEVABLE	
REALISTIC	
TIMLEY	

GOAL	Use space provided to describe your goal.	Goal Range (Circle One)
		Short Term
		Mid-Range
		Long Term

PLAN	Use space provided to explain your plan.

ACTION	Use space provided to list the action steps needed to achieve your goals
	1.
	2.
	3.
	4.
	5.
	6.
	7.
	8.

"If you have a goal in life you should do something every day to achieve it"

Creating a Goal Journal

You should write your goal where you can see it every day. First thing you see when you wake up and the last thing you see before you go to bed. And you should keep a journal of everything you do to achieve that goal. And you should try to write something every day.

WANT TO SHARE YOUR GOAL. USE THE #GFSGOALSFORSUCCESS TO TELL THE WORLD YOUR GOAL

APPENDIX III Time Management

One of the most valuable things you have in your life is time. As a high school student athlete you have a lot of things going on in your life. You have to balance academics, athletics, relationships, family, and possibly a job just to name a few things. So, how do you manage to keep track of all of those things?

Here are some tips that will help you manage your time which will also be very beneficial when you head off to college in a couple of years.

LIST all your activities on a piece of paper. How much time do you spend, on average, completing homework or studying? What organizations do you belong to and when do they meet? What sports are you involved in and when are the practices and games held?

PRIORITIZE. Rank each item to show how important it is and when it needs to be completed.

A. Needs to be done today.
B. Can wait until A tasks are finished.
C. Not that important and can wait until a later time or date.

BE HONEST. You may want to list that History assignment as a C task but if your grades slip we don't see many football games or dances in your future. Keep yourself honest and get the studying done first so you can have fun later on.

Stay **FOCUSED**. The key to a managing your time with a calendar or planner is to stick with it. If it sits in your dresser drawer and never is used, it isn't serving its purpose very well. Make sure to keep at it and keep it up to date. Cross off tasks that have been completed. Reprioritize what hasn't been finished where needed. It sounds complicated now but after a while you'll wonder what you did without it.

Be **FLEXIBLE**. Things change quickly and you may have to move things around a bit to accommodate mom or dad's request to stay home and help with the yard or your siblings. If things change, and you need to miss an activity with a club, etc. let someone in charge know. It'll save you a lot of work later on.

SCHEDULE "ME" TIME. Always remember to make some time for yourself and your friends. A successful student and leader is a well-rounded one! The best suggestion we can make is try it out and see how it goes. If you need to make slight changes or need to come up with your own system...go for it. As long as you keep those commitments, both academic and otherwise, you'll be way ahead of the game.

Please use the weekly calendar on the next page to plan out your day to day activities from your class schedule to practice times to study times. The weekly calendar is a great tool to keep you organized throughout your week.

WEEKLY CALENDAR

	Sunday	Monday	Tuesday	Wednesday	Thursday	Friday	Saturday
8:00							
9:00							
10:00							
11:00							
12:00							
1:00							
2:00							
3:00							
4:00							
5:00							
6:00							
7:00							
8:00							
9:00							
10:00							

APPENDIX IV WEIGHTED PROS CONS LIST

Pro-cons lists are a quick and easy way to analyze a decision. But pro-con lists can be misleading—not all pros and cons have equal importance. Enter the weighted pro-con list. A weighted pro-con lists enable you to indicate how relevant a pro or con is to your decision, by specifying a number to indicate a factor's importance. The higher the number, the greater the factor's importance. Instead of counting the number of pros and cons, add up the weights associated with your pro and con columns. If your pro total exceeds your con total, go forward with the decision. Alternatively, you can subtract your con total from your pro total to create a score for your decision. A Positive score points toward yes decisions, while negative scores point toward no decisions.

Best Practices for Pros Cons List

- **Limit Your Scale**
  Use a scale that gives you the levels of importance you need, but no more. A scale from 1-5 works well.
- **Assign Highest & Lowest Weights First**
  Mark all the pros and cons that are 5's first, then mark all your 1's. Then mark all your 4's in one go, 3's in one go and 2's in one go. By assigning weights one level at a time, you can compare all the factors at that level to see if some should be bumped up or down a level. Ideally all the factors with the same weight should hold the same level of importance to your decision. Mark your highest and lowest weights first, since these are often the easiest to mark off, giving you fewer you need to review for the middle numbers.
- **Ask Why**
  Pro-con lists are about the process as much as the result. Ask yourself why you are assigning the ratings you do. Use pro-con lists as a framework for thinking about your decision, not just a scoring tool.

Appendix Table III – 1 Use the table below to create a Weighted Pros and Cons List (Weight each factor 1-5)

School:				School:			
Weight	Factor	Pros	Cons	Weight	Factor	Pros	Cons
TOTAL							

School:				School:			
Weight	Factor	Pros	Cons	Weight	Factor	Pros	Cons
TOTAL							

APPENDIX V COLLEGE RECRUITING ORGANIZER

The college recruiting process can be a very daunting task but creating a user friendly organizing system will be a useful tool. The Guiding Future Stars College Recruiting Organizer will assist you in managing information on all of the colleges that you are interested in. The CRO will allow you to maintain a school profile with all of the pertinent information about each college and athletics program that you are interested in, as well a place to track any recruiting activities that occur with college coaches.

- **School Profile** including Location, Setting, Size, Tuition, Net Cost, Faculty Student Ratio)
- **Contact information** for head coach and assistant coach
- **Athletics Program** (division, conference, roster size, previous season record)
- **College Recruiting Check List**; you will earn points for completing certain tasks throughout the process.
- **Questions every student-athlete should answer before committing to a school**
- **Recruiting Activities Log**

Tips for Staying Organized throughout the process

- Copies of all the information you have provided to the school – your application, the data sheet you may have to fill out for the coach, the last resume you provided, transcripts, and test scores, etc. By keeping these copies handy, you can easily reproduce them if they are misplaced.
- Just as you organize your paper files, your e-files on your computer should be saved in a way that will allow you to easily refer back to all the documents. Create a folder for each college so that you can readily access the files for any letters, emails, or resumes, you have sent out.
- Maintain your personal calendar to be sure you have added a new event and that you are aware of upcoming deadlines. Try and have your calendar in front of you when you are speaking with a coach on the phone or when you are in a meeting. This will help you to answer questions about your availability for campus visits and evaluations.
- It is essential that you respond to correspondence in a timely manner. You should set regular times where you reply to e-mails, phone calls, and or mail. You want to show coaches you are organized and responsible about deadlines and that you respect their time. College coaches remember the "little things."

Maintaining an organized approach can become very time-consuming and frustrating, especially in the beginning phases of recruiting. Once the system is in place and the process is understood and practiced to perfection, it becomes a tremendous tool for the prospect and the family to use for accurate planning, while increasing the chances of strong success in the college recruiting process.

School Profile	Recruiting Checklist	Date Completed	Points Earned
School	Add School to your list – 10 pts.		
Nickname/Mascot	Learn about school – 10 pts.		
School Colors	Fill out team recruiting questionnaire 30 pts.		
Type of College	Send Intro Email – 50 pts.		
Enrollment	Get a reply from coach – 50 pts.		
Location	Create a Video – 100 pts.		
Setting	Be evaluated by coach – 100 pts.		
Miles from home	Schedule Campus Visit – 50 pts.		
Tuition	Visit campus – 100 pts.		
Avg. Net Cost	Meet with coaching staff – 50 pts.		
Student: Faculty Ratio	Stay overnight on campus – 50 pts.		
Avg. SAT/ACT Scores	Attend ID Camp/Clinic – 100 pts.		
Athletic Program	Ask coach where you stand – 100 pts.		
Division / Conference	Verbal commitment – 200 pts.		
Head Coach	Submit an application – 200 pts.		
Email Address/Phone #	Sign an NLI (DI and DII only) 300 pts.		
Assistant Coach	Get Accepted – 500 pts.		
Email Address/Phone #			
Current Roster Size	Total Points Possible – 2000 pts.		
Previous Season Record	Total Points Earned		
Conference Finish	Goal Range = 1000 – 1500 points		

Recruiting Activity	Date	Notes

College Checklist	Completed	Date	Notes
Campus Tour			
Ate in Dining Hall			
Visited Dormitory			
Visited Athletic Facilities			
Met Coaching Staff			
Stayed Overnight			
Attended a Class			
Met a Professor in your major			
Attended a Practice			
Attended a Game			
Attended a Camp/Clinic			
Submitted an Application			

ACADEMIC / MERIT SCHOLARSHIP OFFER: _____   ATHLETIC SCHOLARSHIP OFFER: _____

Types of Recruiting Activities   Unofficial Visit – Official Visit – Contact – Evaluation – Phone Call – Email – Text Message

Academic Questions	
1. Does the school offer my major?	
2. Is there academic support for student-athletes? Are there required study halls?	
3. Do student-athletes have priority class registration?	
4. Does the school offer summer programs?	
5. What percentage of graduates does the school place into the work force?	
6. What is the graduation rate of the team over the last five years?	
7. What is the attitude of the faculty towards student-athlete's?	
Social Questions	
1. What is male to female ratio?	
2. Do students leave campus for the weekend?	
3. What is on campus housing like? Freshmen? Sophomores? Upperclassmen?	
4. Is on campus housing guaranteed for all four years?	
5. As a student-athlete can I live off campus?	
6. Are there co-ed dorms?	
7. Is there student-athlete housing?	
8. How are the dining facilities? How is the meal plan set up?	

The Top 3 Things I like about this school:

1. _____

2. _____

3. _____

Athletic Questions	
1. What system does the coach play? Defensive? Attacking?	
2. What is your coaching philosophy?	
3. How many players does the team carry? How many players play per game? Travel squad?	
4. How many starters are returning? How many at my position?	
5. What position do you seem me playing in your system? When do you expect me to make an impact?	
6. What is the nature of the conference? Is there a conference tournament?	
7. What are the facilities like? Do you share the facility?	
8. What type of locker room facility do you have? Team Room?	
9. What type of weight room facilities are available?	
10. Do you have a strength and conditioning coach?	
11. Do you lift throughout the season or just in the off-season?	
12. What is your Non-Conference schedule like?	
13. What is attendance at home games?	
14. How do you travel? Bus? Vans? Plane?	
15. Do you have team rules? Who enforces them?	
16. Do you run a pre-season conditioning program? Summer?	
Financial Questions	
1. Are academic scholarships available? Do you combine academic/athletic money?	
2. Am I a scholarship caliber player?	
3. For what reason would I lose my scholarship?	

School Profile	Recruiting Checklist	Date Completed	Points Earned
School	Add School to your list – 10 pts.		
Nickname/Mascot	Learn about school – 10 pts.		
School Colors	Fill out team recruiting questionnaire 30 pts.		
Type of College	Send Intro Email – 50 pts.		
Enrollment	Get a reply from coach – 50 pts.		
Location	Create a Video – 100 pts.		
Setting	Be evaluated by coach – 100 pts.		
Miles from home	Schedule Campus Visit – 50 pts.		
Tuition	Visit campus – 100 pts.		
Avg. Net Cost	Meet with coaching staff – 50 pts.		
Student: Faculty Ratio	Stay overnight on campus – 50 pts.		
Avg. SAT/ACT Scores	Attend ID Camp/Clinic – 100 pts.		
Athletic Program	Ask coach where you stand – 100 pts.		
Division / Conference	Verbal commitment – 200 pts.		
Head Coach	Submit an application – 200 pts.		
Email Address/Phone #	Sign an NLI (DI and DII only) 300 pts.		
Assistant Coach	Get Accepted – 500 pts.		
Email Address/Phone #			
Current Roster Size	Total Points Possible – 2000 pts.		
Previous Season Record	Total Points Earned		
Conference Finish	Goal Range = 1000 – 1500 points		

Recruiting Activity	Date	Notes

College Checklist	Completed	Date	Notes
Campus Tour			
Ate in Dining Hall			
Visited Dormitory			
Visited Athletic Facilities			
Met Coaching Staff			
Stayed Overnight			
Attended a Class			
Met a Professor in your major			
Attended a Practice			
Attended a Game			
Attended a Camp/Clinic			
Submitted an Application			

ACADEMIC / MERIT SCHOLARSHIP OFFER: _____ **ATHLETIC SCHOLARSHIP OFFER:** _____

Types of Recruiting Activities Unofficial Visit – Official Visit – Contact – Evaluation – Phone Call – Email – Text Message

Academic Questions	
1. Does the school offer my major?	
2. Is there academic support for student-athletes? Are there required study halls?	
3. Do student-athletes have priority class registration?	
4. Does the school offer summer programs?	
5. What percentage of graduates does the school place into the work force?	
6. What is the graduation rate of the team over the last five years?	
7. What is the attitude of the faculty towards student-athlete's?	
Social Questions	
1. What is male to female ratio?	
2. Do students leave campus for the weekend?	
3. What is on campus housing like? Freshmen? Sophomores? Upperclassmen?	
4. Is on campus housing guaranteed for all four years?	
5. As a student-athlete can I live off campus?	
6. Are there co-ed dorms?	
7. Is there student-athlete housing?	
8. How are the dining facilities? How is the meal plan set up?	

The Top 3 Things I like about this school:

1. _____

2. _____

3. _____

Athletic Questions	
1. What system does the coach play? Defensive? Attacking?	
2. What is your coaching philosophy?	
3. How many players does the team carry? How many players play per game? Travel squad?	
4. How many starters are returning? How many at my position?	
5. What position do you seem me playing in your system? When do you expect me to make an impact?	
6. What is the nature of the conference? Is there a conference tournament?	
7. What are the facilities like? Do you share the facility?	
8. What type of locker room facility do you have? Team Room?	
9. What type of weight room facilities are available?	
10. Do you have a strength and conditioning coach?	
11. Do you lift throughout the season or just in the off-season?	
12. What is your Non-Conference schedule like?	
13. What is attendance at home games?	
14. How do you travel? Bus? Vans? Plane?	
15. Do you have team rules? Who enforces them?	
16. Do you run a pre-season conditioning program? Summer?	
Financial Questions	
1. Are academic scholarships available? Do you combine academic/athletic money?	
2. Am I a scholarship caliber player?	
3. For what reason would I lose my scholarship?	

School Profile	Recruiting Checklist	Date Completed	Points Earned
School	Add School to your list – 10 pts.		
Nickname/Mascot	Learn about school – 10 pts.		
School Colors	Fill out team recruiting questionnaire 30 pts.		
Type of College	Send Intro Email – 50 pts.		
Enrollment	Get a reply from coach – 50 pts.		
Location	Create a Video – 100 pts.		
Setting	Be evaluated by coach – 100 pts.		
Miles from home	Schedule Campus Visit – 50 pts.		
Tuition	Visit campus – 100 pts.		
Avg. Net Cost	Meet with coaching staff – 50 pts.		
Student: Faculty Ratio	Stay overnight on campus – 50 pts.		
Avg. SAT/ACT Scores	Attend ID Camp/Clinic – 100 pts.		
Athletic Program	Ask coach where you stand – 100 pts.		
Division / Conference	Verbal commitment – 200 pts.		
Head Coach	Submit an application – 200 pts.		
Email Address/Phone #	Sign an NLI (DI and DII only) 300 pts.		
Assistant Coach	Get Accepted – 500 pts.		
Email Address/Phone #			
Current Roster Size	Total Points Possible – 2000 pts.		
Previous Season Record	Total Points Earned		
Conference Finish	Goal Range = 1000 – 1500 points		

Recruiting Activity	Date	Notes

College Checklist	Completed	Date	Notes
Campus Tour			
Ate in Dining Hall			
Visited Dormitory			
Visited Athletic Facilities			
Met Coaching Staff			
Stayed Overnight			
Attended a Class			
Met a Professor in your major			
Attended a Practice			
Attended a Game			
Attended a Camp/Clinic			
Submitted an Application			

ACADEMIC / MERIT SCHOLARSHIP OFFER: _____ **ATHLETIC SCHOLARSHIP OFFER:** _____

Types of Recruiting Activities   Unofficial Visit – Official Visit – Contact – Evaluation – Phone Call – Email – Text Message

Academic Questions	
1. Does the school offer my major?	
2. Is there academic support for student-athletes? Are there required study halls?	
3. Do student-athletes have priority class registration?	
4. Does the school offer summer programs?	
5. What percentage of graduates does the school place into the work force?	
6. What is the graduation rate of the team over the last five years?	
7. What is the attitude of the faculty towards student-athlete's?	
Social Questions	
1. What is male to female ratio?	
2. Do students leave campus for the weekend?	
3. What is on campus housing like? Freshmen? Sophomores? Upperclassmen?	
4. Is on campus housing guaranteed for all four years?	
5. As a student-athlete can I live off campus?	
6. Are there co-ed dorms?	
7. Is there student-athlete housing?	
8. How are the dining facilities? How is the meal plan set up?	

The Top 3 Things I like about this school:

1. _____

2. _____

3. _____

Athletic Questions	
1. What system does the coach play? Defensive? Attacking?	
2. What is your coaching philosophy?	
3. How many players does the team carry? How many players play per game? Travel squad?	
4. How many starters are returning? How many at my position?	
5. What position do you seem me playing in your system? When do you expect me to make an impact?	
6. What is the nature of the conference? Is there a conference tournament?	
7. What are the facilities like? Do you share the facility?	
8. What type of locker room facility do you have? Team Room?	
9. What type of weight room facilities are available?	
10. Do you have a strength and conditioning coach?	
11. Do you lift throughout the season or just in the off-season?	
12. What is your Non-Conference schedule like?	
13. What is attendance at home games?	
14. How do you travel? Bus? Vans? Plane?	
15. Do you have team rules? Who enforces them?	
16. Do you run a pre-season conditioning program? Summer?	
Financial Questions	
1. Are academic scholarships available? Do you combine academic/athletic money?	
2. Am I a scholarship caliber player?	
3. For what reason would I lose my scholarship?	

School Profile	Recruiting Checklist	Date Completed	Points Earned
School	Add School to your list – 10 pts.		
Nickname/Mascot	Learn about school – 10 pts.		
School Colors	Fill out team recruiting questionnaire 30 pts.		
Type of College	Send Intro Email – 50 pts.		
Enrollment	Get a reply from coach – 50 pts.		
Location	Create a Video – 100 pts.		
Setting	Be evaluated by coach – 100 pts.		
Miles from home	Schedule Campus Visit – 50 pts.		
Tuition	Visit campus – 100 pts.		
Avg. Net Cost	Meet with coaching staff – 50 pts.		
Student: Faculty Ratio	Stay overnight on campus – 50 pts.		
Avg. SAT/ACT Scores	Attend ID Camp/Clinic – 100 pts.		
Athletic Program	Ask coach where you stand – 100 pts.		
Division / Conference	Verbal commitment – 200 pts.		
Head Coach	Submit an application – 200 pts.		
Email Address/Phone #	Sign an NLI (DI and DII only) 300 pts.		
Assistant Coach	Get Accepted – 500 pts.		
Email Address/Phone #			
Current Roster Size	Total Points Possible – 2000 pts.		
Previous Season Record	Total Points Earned		
Conference Finish	Goal Range = 1000 – 1500 points		

Recruiting Activity	Date	Notes

College Checklist	Completed	Date	Notes
Campus Tour			
Ate in Dining Hall			
Visited Dormitory			
Visited Athletic Facilities			
Met Coaching Staff			
Stayed Overnight			
Attended a Class			
Met a Professor in your major			
Attended a Practice			
Attended a Game			
Attended a Camp/Clinic			
Submitted an Application			

ACADEMIC / MERIT SCHOLARSHIP OFFER: _____

ATHLETIC SCHOLARSHIP OFFER: _____

Types of Recruiting Activities   Unofficial Visit – Official Visit – Contact – Evaluation – Phone Call – Email – Text Message

Academic Questions	
1. Does the school offer my major?	
2. Is there academic support for student-athletes? Are there required study halls?	
3. Do student-athletes have priority class registration?	
4. Does the school offer summer programs?	
5. What percentage of graduates does the school place into the work force?	
6. What is the graduation rate of the team over the last five years?	
7. What is the attitude of the faculty towards student-athlete's?	
Social Questions	
1. What is male to female ratio?	
2. Do students leave campus for the weekend?	
3. What is on campus housing like? Freshmen? Sophomores? Upperclassmen?	
4. Is on campus housing guaranteed for all four years?	
5. As a student-athlete can I live off campus?	
6. Are there co-ed dorms?	
7. Is there student-athlete housing?	
8. How are the dining facilities? How is the meal plan set up?	

The Top 3 Things I like about this school:

1. _____

2. _____

3. _____

Athletic Questions	
1. What system does the coach play? Defensive? Attacking?	
2. What is your coaching philosophy?	
3. How many players does the team carry? How many players play per game? Travel squad?	
4. How many starters are returning? How many at my position?	
5. What position do you seem me playing in your system? When do you expect me to make an impact?	
6. What is the nature of the conference? Is there a conference tournament?	
7. What are the facilities like? Do you share the facility?	
8. What type of locker room facility do you have? Team Room?	
9. What type of weight room facilities are available?	
10. Do you have a strength and conditioning coach?	
11. Do you lift throughout the season or just in the off-season?	
12. What is your Non-Conference schedule like?	
13. What is attendance at home games?	
14. How do you travel? Bus? Vans? Plane?	
15. Do you have team rules? Who enforces them?	
16. Do you run a pre-season conditioning program? Summer?	
Financial Questions	
1. Are academic scholarships available? Do you combine academic/athletic money?	
2. Am I a scholarship caliber player?	
3. For what reason would I lose my scholarship?	

School Profile		Recruiting Checklist	Date Completed	Points Earned
School		Add School to your list – 10 pts.		
Nickname/Mascot		Learn about school – 10 pts.		
School Colors		Fill out team recruiting questionnaire 30 pts.		
Type of College		Send Intro Email – 50 pts.		
Enrollment		Get a reply from coach – 50 pts.		
Location		Create a Video – 100 pts.		
Setting		Be evaluated by coach – 100 pts.		
Miles from home		Schedule Campus Visit – 50 pts.		
Tuition		Visit campus – 100 pts.		
Avg. Net Cost		Meet with coaching staff – 50 pts.		
Student: Faculty Ratio		Stay overnight on campus – 50 pts.		
Avg. SAT/ACT Scores		Attend ID Camp/Clinic – 100 pts.		
Athletic Program		Ask coach where you stand – 100 pts.		
Division / Conference		Verbal commitment – 200 pts.		
Head Coach		Submit an application – 200 pts.		
Email Address/Phone #		Sign an NLI (DI and DII only) 300 pts.		
Assistant Coach		Get Accepted – 500 pts.		
Email Address/Phone #				
Current Roster Size		Total Points Possible – 2000 pts.		
Previous Season Record		Total Points Earned		
Conference Finish		Goal Range = 1000 – 1500 points		

Recruiting Activity	Date	Notes

College Checklist	Completed	Date	Notes
Campus Tour			
Ate in Dining Hall			
Visited Dormitory			
Visited Athletic Facilities			
Met Coaching Staff			
Stayed Overnight			
Attended a Class			
Met a Professor in your major			
Attended a Practice			
Attended a Game			
Attended a Camp/Clinic			
Submitted an Application			

ACADEMIC / MERIT SCHOLARSHIP OFFER: _____ **ATHLETIC SCHOLARSHIP OFFER:** _____

Types of Recruiting Activities   Unofficial Visit – Official Visit – Contact – Evaluation – Phone Call – Email – Text Message

Academic Questions	
1. Does the school offer my major?	
2. Is there academic support for student-athletes? Are there required study halls?	
3. Do student-athletes have priority class registration?	
4. Does the school offer summer programs?	
5. What percentage of graduates does the school place into the work force?	
6. What is the graduation rate of the team over the last five years?	
7. What is the attitude of the faculty towards student-athlete's?	
Social Questions	
1. What is male to female ratio?	
2. Do students leave campus for the weekend?	
3. What is on campus housing like? Freshmen? Sophomores? Upperclassmen?	
4. Is on campus housing guaranteed for all four years?	
5. As a student-athlete can I live off campus?	
6. Are there co-ed dorms?	
7. Is there student-athlete housing?	
8. How are the dining facilities? How is the meal plan set up?	

The Top 3 Things I like about this school:

1. _____

2. _____

3. _____

Athletic Questions	
1. What system does the coach play? Defensive? Attacking?	
2. What is your coaching philosophy?	
3. How many players does the team carry? How many players play per game? Travel squad?	
4. How many starters are returning? How many at my position?	
5. What position do you seem me playing in your system? When do you expect me to make an impact?	
6. What is the nature of the conference? Is there a conference tournament?	
7. What are the facilities like? Do you share the facility?	
8. What type of locker room facility do you have? Team Room?	
9. What type of weight room facilities are available?	
10. Do you have a strength and conditioning coach?	
11. Do you lift throughout the season or just in the off-season?	
12. What is your Non-Conference schedule like?	
13. What is attendance at home games?	
14. How do you travel? Bus? Vans? Plane?	
15. Do you have team rules? Who enforces them?	
16. Do you run a pre-season conditioning program? Summer?	
Financial Questions	
1. Are academic scholarships available? Do you combine academic/athletic money?	
2. Am I a scholarship caliber player?	
3. For what reason would I lose my scholarship?	

School Profile	Recruiting Checklist	Date Completed	Points Earned
School	Add School to your list – 10 pts.		
Nickname/Mascot	Learn about school – 10 pts.		
School Colors	Fill out team recruiting questionnaire 30 pts.		
Type of College	Send Intro Email – 50 pts.		
Enrollment	Get a reply from coach – 50 pts.		
Location	Create a Video – 100 pts.		
Setting	Be evaluated by coach – 100 pts.		
Miles from home	Schedule Campus Visit – 50 pts.		
Tuition	Visit campus – 100 pts.		
Avg. Net Cost	Meet with coaching staff – 50 pts.		
Student: Faculty Ratio	Stay overnight on campus – 50 pts.		
Avg. SAT/ACT Scores	Attend ID Camp/Clinic – 100 pts.		
Athletic Program	Ask coach where you stand – 100 pts.		
Division / Conference	Verbal commitment – 200 pts.		
Head Coach	Submit an application – 200 pts.		
Email Address/Phone #	Sign an NLI (DI and DII only) 300 pts.		
Assistant Coach	Get Accepted – 500 pts.		
Email Address/Phone #			
Current Roster Size	Total Points Possible – 2000 pts.		
Previous Season Record	Total Points Earned		
Conference Finish	Goal Range = 1000 – 1500 points		

Recruiting Activity	Date	Notes

College Checklist	Completed	Date	Notes
Campus Tour			
Ate in Dining Hall			
Visited Dormitory			
Visited Athletic Facilities			
Met Coaching Staff			
Stayed Overnight			
Attended a Class			
Met a Professor in your major			
Attended a Practice			
Attended a Game			
Attended a Camp/Clinic			
Submitted an Application			

ACADEMIC / MERIT SCHOLARSHIP OFFER: _____   **ATHLETIC SCHOLARSHIP OFFER:** _____

Types of Recruiting Activities   Unofficial Visit – Official Visit – Contact – Evaluation – Phone Call – Email – Text Message

Academic Questions	
1. Does the school offer my major?	
2. Is there academic support for student-athletes? Are there required study halls?	
3. Do student-athletes have priority class registration?	
4. Does the school offer summer programs?	
5. What percentage of graduates does the school place into the work force?	
6. What is the graduation rate of the team over the last five years?	
7. What is the attitude of the faculty towards student-athlete's?	
Social Questions	
1. What is male to female ratio?	
2. Do students leave campus for the weekend?	
3. What is on campus housing like? Freshmen? Sophomores? Upperclassmen?	
4. Is on campus housing guaranteed for all four years?	
5. As a student-athlete can I live off campus?	
6. Are there co-ed dorms?	
7. Is there student-athlete housing?	
8. How are the dining facilities? How is the meal plan set up?	

The Top 3 Things I like about this school:

1. _____

2. _____

3. _____

Athletic Questions	
1. What system does the coach play? Defensive? Attacking?	
2. What is your coaching philosophy?	
3. How many players does the team carry? How many players play per game? Travel squad?	
4. How many starters are returning? How many at my position?	
5. What position do you seem me playing in your system? When do you expect me to make an impact?	
6. What is the nature of the conference? Is there a conference tournament?	
7. What are the facilities like? Do you share the facility?	
8. What type of locker room facility do you have? Team Room?	
9. What type of weight room facilities are available?	
10. Do you have a strength and conditioning coach?	
11. Do you lift throughout the season or just in the off-season?	
12. What is your Non-Conference schedule like?	
13. What is attendance at home games?	
14. How do you travel? Bus? Vans? Plane?	
15. Do you have team rules? Who enforces them?	
16. Do you run a pre-season conditioning program? Summer?	
Financial Questions	
1. Are academic scholarships available? Do you combine academic/athletic money?	
2. Am I a scholarship caliber player?	
3. For what reason would I lose my scholarship?	

School Profile		Recruiting Checklist	Date Completed	Points Earned
School		Add School to your list – 10 pts.		
Nickname/Mascot		Learn about school – 10 pts.		
School Colors		Fill out team recruiting questionnaire 30 pts.		
Type of College		Send Intro Email – 50 pts.		
Enrollment		Get a reply from coach – 50 pts.		
Location		Create a Video – 100 pts.		
Setting		Be evaluated by coach – 100 pts.		
Miles from home		Schedule Campus Visit – 50 pts.		
Tuition		Visit campus – 100 pts.		
Avg. Net Cost		Meet with coaching staff – 50 pts.		
Student: Faculty Ratio		Stay overnight on campus – 50 pts.		
Avg. SAT/ACT Scores		Attend ID Camp/Clinic – 100 pts.		
Athletic Program		Ask coach where you stand – 100 pts.		
Division / Conference		Verbal commitment – 200 pts.		
Head Coach		Submit an application – 200 pts.		
Email Address/Phone #		Sign an NLI (DI and DII only) 300 pts.		
Assistant Coach		Get Accepted – 500 pts.		
Email Address/Phone #				
Current Roster Size		Total Points Possible – 2000 pts.		
Previous Season Record		Total Points Earned		
Conference Finish		Goal Range = 1000 – 1500 points		

Recruiting Activity	Date	Notes

College Checklist	Completed	Date	Notes
Campus Tour			
Ate in Dining Hall			
Visited Dormitory			
Visited Athletic Facilities			
Met Coaching Staff			
Stayed Overnight			
Attended a Class			
Met a Professor in your major			
Attended a Practice			
Attended a Game			
Attended a Camp/Clinic			
Submitted an Application			

ACADEMIC / MERIT SCHOLARSHIP OFFER: _____ **ATHLETIC SCHOLARSHIP OFFER:** _____

Types of Recruiting Activities Unofficial Visit – Official Visit – Contact – Evaluation – Phone Call – Email – Text Message

Academic Questions	
1. Does the school offer my major?	
2. Is there academic support for student-athletes? Are there required study halls?	
3. Do student-athletes have priority class registration?	
4. Does the school offer summer programs?	
5. What percentage of graduates does the school place into the work force?	
6. What is the graduation rate of the team over the last five years?	
7. What is the attitude of the faculty towards student-athlete's?	
Social Questions	
1. What is male to female ratio?	
2. Do students leave campus for the weekend?	
3. What is on campus housing like? Freshmen? Sophomores? Upperclassmen?	
4. Is on campus housing guaranteed for all four years?	
5. As a student-athlete can I live off campus?	
6. Are there co-ed dorms?	
7. Is there student-athlete housing?	
8. How are the dining facilities? How is the meal plan set up?	

The Top 3 Things I like about this school:

1. _____

2. _____

3. _____

Athletic Questions	
1. What system does the coach play? Defensive? Attacking?	
2. What is your coaching philosophy?	
3. How many players does the team carry? How many players play per game? Travel squad?	
4. How many starters are returning? How many at my position?	
5. What position do you seem me playing in your system? When do you expect me to make an impact?	
6. What is the nature of the conference? Is there a conference tournament?	
7. What are the facilities like? Do you share the facility?	
8. What type of locker room facility do you have? Team Room?	
9. What type of weight room facilities are available?	
10. Do you have a strength and conditioning coach?	
11. Do you lift throughout the season or just in the off-season?	
12. What is your Non-Conference schedule like?	
13. What is attendance at home games?	
14. How do you travel? Bus? Vans? Plane?	
15. Do you have team rules? Who enforces them?	
16. Do you run a pre-season conditioning program? Summer?	
Financial Questions	
1. Are academic scholarships available? Do you combine academic/athletic money?	
2. Am I a scholarship caliber player?	
3. For what reason would I lose my scholarship?	

School Profile		Recruiting Checklist	Date Completed	Points Earned
School		Add School to your list – 10 pts.		
Nickname/Mascot		Learn about school – 10 pts.		
School Colors		Fill out team recruiting questionnaire 30 pts.		
Type of College		Send Intro Email – 50 pts.		
Enrollment		Get a reply from coach – 50 pts.		
Location		Create a Video – 100 pts.		
Setting		Be evaluated by coach – 100 pts.		
Miles from home		Schedule Campus Visit – 50 pts.		
Tuition		Visit campus – 100 pts.		
Avg. Net Cost		Meet with coaching staff – 50 pts.		
Student: Faculty Ratio		Stay overnight on campus – 50 pts.		
Avg. SAT/ACT Scores		Attend ID Camp/Clinic – 100 pts.		
Athletic Program		Ask coach where you stand – 100 pts.		
Division / Conference		Verbal commitment – 200 pts.		
Head Coach		Submit an application – 200 pts.		
Email Address/Phone #		Sign an NLI (DI and DII only) 300 pts.		
Assistant Coach		Get Accepted – 500 pts.		
Email Address/Phone #				
Current Roster Size		Total Points Possible – 2000 pts.		
Previous Season Record		Total Points Earned		
Conference Finish		Goal Range = 1000 – 1500 points		

Recruiting Activity	Date	Notes

College Checklist	Completed	Date	Notes
Campus Tour			
Ate in Dining Hall			
Visited Dormitory			
Visited Athletic Facilities			
Met Coaching Staff			
Stayed Overnight			
Attended a Class			
Met a Professor in your major			
Attended a Practice			
Attended a Game			
Attended a Camp/Clinic			
Submitted an Application			

ACADEMIC / MERIT SCHOLARSHIP OFFER: _____ ATHLETIC SCHOLARSHIP OFFER: _____

Types of Recruiting Activities Unofficial Visit – Official Visit – Contact – Evaluation – Phone Call – Email – Text Message

Academic Questions	
1. Does the school offer my major?	
2. Is there academic support for student-athletes? Are there required study halls?	
3. Do student-athletes have priority class registration?	
4. Does the school offer summer programs?	
5. What percentage of graduates does the school place into the work force?	
6. What is the graduation rate of the team over the last five years?	
7. What is the attitude of the faculty towards student-athlete's?	
Social Questions	
1. What is male to female ratio?	
2. Do students leave campus for the weekend?	
3. What is on campus housing like? Freshmen? Sophomores? Upperclassmen?	
4. Is on campus housing guaranteed for all four years?	
5. As a student-athlete can I live off campus?	
6. Are there co-ed dorms?	
7. Is there student-athlete housing?	
8. How are the dining facilities? How is the meal plan set up?	

The Top 3 Things I like about this school:

1. _____

2. _____

3. _____

Athletic Questions	
1. What system does the coach play? Defensive? Attacking?	
2. What is your coaching philosophy?	
3. How many players does the team carry? How many players play per game? Travel squad?	
4. How many starters are returning? How many at my position?	
5. What position do you seem me playing in your system? When do you expect me to make an impact?	
6. What is the nature of the conference? Is there a conference tournament?	
7. What are the facilities like? Do you share the facility?	
8. What type of locker room facility do you have? Team Room?	
9. What type of weight room facilities are available?	
10. Do you have a strength and conditioning coach?	
11. Do you lift throughout the season or just in the off-season?	
12. What is your Non-Conference schedule like?	
13. What is attendance at home games?	
14. How do you travel? Bus? Vans? Plane?	
15. Do you have team rules? Who enforces them?	
16. Do you run a pre-season conditioning program? Summer?	
Financial Questions	
1. Are academic scholarships available? Do you combine academic/athletic money?	
2. Am I a scholarship caliber player?	
3. For what reason would I lose my scholarship?	

School Profile		Recruiting Checklist	Date Completed	Points Earned
School		Add School to your list – 10 pts.		
Nickname/Mascot		Learn about school – 10 pts.		
School Colors		Fill out team recruiting questionnaire 30 pts.		
Type of College		Send Intro Email – 50 pts.		
Enrollment		Get a reply from coach – 50 pts.		
Location		Create a Video – 100 pts.		
Setting		Be evaluated by coach – 100 pts.		
Miles from home		Schedule Campus Visit – 50 pts.		
Tuition		Visit campus – 100 pts.		
Avg. Net Cost		Meet with coaching staff – 50 pts.		
Student: Faculty Ratio		Stay overnight on campus – 50 pts.		
Avg. SAT/ACT Scores		Attend ID Camp/Clinic – 100 pts.		
Athletic Program		Ask coach where you stand – 100 pts.		
Division / Conference		Verbal commitment – 200 pts.		
Head Coach		Submit an application – 200 pts.		
Email Address/Phone #		Sign an NLI (DI and DII only) 300 pts.		
Assistant Coach		Get Accepted – 500 pts.		
Email Address/Phone #				
Current Roster Size		Total Points Possible – 2000 pts.		
Previous Season Record		Total Points Earned		
Conference Finish		Goal Range = 1000 – 1500 points		

Recruiting Activity	Date	Notes

College Checklist	Completed	Date	Notes
Campus Tour			
Ate in Dining Hall			
Visited Dormitory			
Visited Athletic Facilities			
Met Coaching Staff			
Stayed Overnight			
Attended a Class			
Met a Professor in your major			
Attended a Practice			
Attended a Game			
Attended a Camp/Clinic			
Submitted an Application			

ACADEMIC / MERIT SCHOLARSHIP OFFER: _____

ATHLETIC SCHOLARSHIP OFFER: _____

Types of Recruiting Activities   Unofficial Visit – Official Visit – Contact – Evaluation – Phone Call – Email – Text Message

Academic Questions	
1. Does the school offer my major?	
2. Is there academic support for student-athletes? Are there required study halls?	
3. Do student-athletes have priority class registration?	
4. Does the school offer summer programs?	
5. What percentage of graduates does the school place into the work force?	
6. What is the graduation rate of the team over the last five years?	
7. What is the attitude of the faculty towards student-athlete's?	
Social Questions	
1. What is male to female ratio?	
2. Do students leave campus for the weekend?	
3. What is on campus housing like? Freshmen? Sophomores? Upperclassmen?	
4. Is on campus housing guaranteed for all four years?	
5. As a student-athlete can I live off campus?	
6. Are there co-ed dorms?	
7. Is there student-athlete housing?	
8. How are the dining facilities? How is the meal plan set up?	

The Top 3 Things I like about this school:

1. _____

2. _____

3. _____

Athletic Questions	
1. What system does the coach play? Defensive? Attacking?	
2. What is your coaching philosophy?	
3. How many players does the team carry? How many players play per game? Travel squad?	
4. How many starters are returning? How many at my position?	
5. What position do you seem me playing in your system? When do you expect me to make an impact?	
6. What is the nature of the conference? Is there a conference tournament?	
7. What are the facilities like? Do you share the facility?	
8. What type of locker room facility do you have? Team Room?	
9. What type of weight room facilities are available?	
10. Do you have a strength and conditioning coach?	
11. Do you lift throughout the season or just in the off-season?	
12. What is your Non-Conference schedule like?	
13. What is attendance at home games?	
14. How do you travel? Bus? Vans? Plane?	
15. Do you have team rules? Who enforces them?	
16. Do you run a pre-season conditioning program? Summer?	
Financial Questions	
1. Are academic scholarships available? Do you combine academic/athletic money?	
2. Am I a scholarship caliber player?	
3. For what reason would I lose my scholarship?	

School Profile	Recruiting Checklist	Date Completed	Points Earned
School	Add School to your list – 10 pts.		
Nickname/Mascot	Learn about school – 10 pts.		
School Colors	Fill out team recruiting questionnaire 30 pts.		
Type of College	Send Intro Email – 50 pts.		
Enrollment	Get a reply from coach – 50 pts.		
Location	Create a Video – 100 pts.		
Setting	Be evaluated by coach – 100 pts.		
Miles from home	Schedule Campus Visit – 50 pts.		
Tuition	Visit campus – 100 pts.		
Avg. Net Cost	Meet with coaching staff – 50 pts.		
Student: Faculty Ratio	Stay overnight on campus – 50 pts.		
Avg. SAT/ACT Scores	Attend ID Camp/Clinic – 100 pts.		
Athletic Program	Ask coach where you stand – 100 pts.		
Division / Conference	Verbal commitment – 200 pts.		
Head Coach	Submit an application – 200 pts.		
Email Address/Phone #	Sign an NLI (DI and DII only) 300 pts.		
Assistant Coach	Get Accepted – 500 pts.		
Email Address/Phone #			
Current Roster Size	Total Points Possible – 2000 pts.		
Previous Season Record	Total Points Earned		
Conference Finish	Goal Range = 1000 – 1500 points		

Recruiting Activity	Date	Notes

College Checklist	Completed	Date	Notes
Campus Tour			
Ate in Dining Hall			
Visited Dormitory			
Visited Athletic Facilities			
Met Coaching Staff			
Stayed Overnight			
Attended a Class			
Met a Professor in your major			
Attended a Practice			
Attended a Game			
Attended a Camp/Clinic			
Submitted an Application			

ACADEMIC / MERIT SCHOLARSHIP OFFER: _____ **ATHLETIC SCHOLARSHIP OFFER:** _____

Types of Recruiting Activities   Unofficial Visit – Official Visit – Contact – Evaluation – Phone Call – Email – Text Message

Academic Questions	
1. Does the school offer my major?	
2. Is there academic support for student-athletes? Are there required study halls?	
3. Do student-athletes have priority class registration?	
4. Does the school offer summer programs?	
5. What percentage of graduates does the school place into the work force?	
6. What is the graduation rate of the team over the last five years?	
7. What is the attitude of the faculty towards student-athlete's?	
Social Questions	
1. What is male to female ratio?	
2. Do students leave campus for the weekend?	
3. What is on campus housing like? Freshmen? Sophomores? Upperclassmen?	
4. Is on campus housing guaranteed for all four years?	
5. As a student-athlete can I live off campus?	
6. Are there co-ed dorms?	
7. Is there student-athlete housing?	
8. How are the dining facilities? How is the meal plan set up?	

The Top 3 Things I like about this school:

1. _____

2. _____

3. _____

Athletic Questions	
1. What system does the coach play? Defensive? Attacking?	
2. What is your coaching philosophy?	
3. How many players does the team carry? How many players play per game? Travel squad?	
4. How many starters are returning? How many at my position?	
5. What position do you seem me playing in your system? When do you expect me to make an impact?	
6. What is the nature of the conference? Is there a conference tournament?	
7. What are the facilities like? Do you share the facility?	
8. What type of locker room facility do you have? Team Room?	
9. What type of weight room facilities are available?	
10. Do you have a strength and conditioning coach?	
11. Do you lift throughout the season or just in the off-season?	
12. What is your Non-Conference schedule like?	
13. What is attendance at home games?	
14. How do you travel? Bus? Vans? Plane?	
15. Do you have team rules? Who enforces them?	
16. Do you run a pre-season conditioning program? Summer?	
Financial Questions	
1. Are academic scholarships available? Do you combine academic/athletic money?	
2. Am I a scholarship caliber player?	
3. For what reason would I lose my scholarship?	

School Profile		Recruiting Checklist	Date Completed	Points Earned
School		Add School to your list – 10 pts.		
Nickname/Mascot		Learn about school – 10 pts.		
School Colors		Fill out team recruiting questionnaire 30 pts.		
Type of College		Send Intro Email – 50 pts.		
Enrollment		Get a reply from coach – 50 pts.		
Location		Create a Video – 100 pts.		
Setting		Be evaluated by coach – 100 pts.		
Miles from home		Schedule Campus Visit – 50 pts.		
Tuition		Visit campus – 100 pts.		
Avg. Net Cost		Meet with coaching staff – 50 pts.		
Student: Faculty Ratio		Stay overnight on campus – 50 pts.		
Avg. SAT/ACT Scores		Attend ID Camp/Clinic – 100 pts.		
Athletic Program		Ask coach where you stand – 100 pts.		
Division / Conference		Verbal commitment – 200 pts.		
Head Coach		Submit an application – 200 pts.		
Email Address/Phone #		Sign an NLI (DI and DII only) 300 pts.		
Assistant Coach		Get Accepted – 500 pts.		
Email Address/Phone #				
Current Roster Size		Total Points Possible – 2000 pts.		
Previous Season Record		Total Points Earned		
Conference Finish		Goal Range = 1000 – 1500 points		

Recruiting Activity	Date	Notes

College Checklist	Completed	Date	Notes
Campus Tour			
Ate in Dining Hall			
Visited Dormitory			
Visited Athletic Facilities			
Met Coaching Staff			
Stayed Overnight			
Attended a Class			
Met a Professor in your major			
Attended a Practice			
Attended a Game			
Attended a Camp/Clinic			
Submitted an Application			

ACADEMIC / MERIT SCHOLARSHIP OFFER: _____ **ATHLETIC SCHOLARSHIP OFFER:** _____

Types of Recruiting Activities   Unofficial Visit – Official Visit – Contact – Evaluation – Phone Call – Email – Text Message

Academic Questions	
1. Does the school offer my major?	
2. Is there academic support for student-athletes? Are there required study halls?	
3. Do student-athletes have priority class registration?	
4. Does the school offer summer programs?	
5. What percentage of graduates does the school place into the work force?	
6. What is the graduation rate of the team over the last five years?	
7. What is the attitude of the faculty towards student-athlete's?	
Social Questions	
1. What is male to female ratio?	
2. Do students leave campus for the weekend?	
3. What is on campus housing like? Freshmen? Sophomores? Upperclassmen?	
4. Is on campus housing guaranteed for all four years?	
5. As a student-athlete can I live off campus?	
6. Are there co-ed dorms?	
7. Is there student-athlete housing?	
8. How are the dining facilities? How is the meal plan set up?	

The Top 3 Things I like about this school:

1. _____

2. _____

3. _____

Athletic Questions	
1. What system does the coach play? Defensive? Attacking?	
2. What is your coaching philosophy?	
3. How many players does the team carry? How many players play per game? Travel squad?	
4. How many starters are returning? How many at my position?	
5. What position do you seem me playing in your system? When do you expect me to make an impact?	
6. What is the nature of the conference? Is there a conference tournament?	
7. What are the facilities like? Do you share the facility?	
8. What type of locker room facility do you have? Team Room?	
9. What type of weight room facilities are available?	
10. Do you have a strength and conditioning coach?	
11. Do you lift throughout the season or just in the off-season?	
12. What is your Non-Conference schedule like?	
13. What is attendance at home games?	
14. How do you travel? Bus? Vans? Plane?	
15. Do you have team rules? Who enforces them?	
16. Do you run a pre-season conditioning program? Summer?	
Financial Questions	
1. Are academic scholarships available? Do you combine academic/athletic money?	
2. Am I a scholarship caliber player?	
3. For what reason would I lose my scholarship?	

School Profile	Recruiting Checklist	Date Completed	Points Earned
School	Add School to your list – 10 pts.		
Nickname/Mascot	Learn about school – 10 pts.		
School Colors	Fill out team recruiting questionnaire 30 pts.		
Type of College	Send Intro Email – 50 pts.		
Enrollment	Get a reply from coach – 50 pts.		
Location	Create a Video – 100 pts.		
Setting	Be evaluated by coach – 100 pts.		
Miles from home	Schedule Campus Visit – 50 pts.		
Tuition	Visit campus – 100 pts.		
Avg. Net Cost	Meet with coaching staff – 50 pts.		
Student: Faculty Ratio	Stay overnight on campus – 50 pts.		
Avg. SAT/ACT Scores	Attend ID Camp/Clinic – 100 pts.		
Athletic Program	Ask coach where you stand – 100 pts.		
Division / Conference	Verbal commitment – 200 pts.		
Head Coach	Submit an application – 200 pts.		
Email Address/Phone #	Sign an NLI (DI and DII only) 300 pts.		
Assistant Coach	Get Accepted – 500 pts.		
Email Address/Phone #			
Current Roster Size	Total Points Possible – 2000 pts.		
Previous Season Record	Total Points Earned		
Conference Finish	Goal Range = 1000 – 1500 points		

Recruiting Activity	Date	Notes

College Checklist	Completed	Date	Notes
Campus Tour			
Ate in Dining Hall			
Visited Dormitory			
Visited Athletic Facilities			
Met Coaching Staff			
Stayed Overnight			
Attended a Class			
Met a Professor in your major			
Attended a Practice			
Attended a Game			
Attended a Camp/Clinic			
Submitted an Application			

ACADEMIC / MERIT SCHOLARSHIP OFFER: _____ **ATHLETIC SCHOLARSHIP OFFER:** _____

Types of Recruiting Activities   Unofficial Visit – Official Visit – Contact – Evaluation – Phone Call – Email – Text Message

Academic Questions	
1. Does the school offer my major?	
2. Is there academic support for student-athletes? Are there required study halls?	
3. Do student-athletes have priority class registration?	
4. Does the school offer summer programs?	
5. What percentage of graduates does the school place into the work force?	
6. What is the graduation rate of the team over the last five years?	
7. What is the attitude of the faculty towards student-athlete's?	
Social Questions	
1. What is male to female ratio?	
2. Do students leave campus for the weekend?	
3. What is on campus housing like? Freshmen? Sophomores? Upperclassmen?	
4. Is on campus housing guaranteed for all four years?	
5. As a student-athlete can I live off campus?	
6. Are there co-ed dorms?	
7. Is there student-athlete housing?	
8. How are the dining facilities? How is the meal plan set up?	

The Top 3 Things I like about this school:

1. _____

2. _____

3. _____

Athletic Questions	
1. What system does the coach play? Defensive? Attacking?	
2. What is your coaching philosophy?	
3. How many players does the team carry? How many players play per game? Travel squad?	
4. How many starters are returning? How many at my position?	
5. What position do you seem me playing in your system? When do you expect me to make an impact?	
6. What is the nature of the conference? Is there a conference tournament?	
7. What are the facilities like? Do you share the facility?	
8. What type of locker room facility do you have? Team Room?	
9. What type of weight room facilities are available?	
10. Do you have a strength and conditioning coach?	
11. Do you lift throughout the season or just in the off-season?	
12. What is your Non-Conference schedule like?	
13. What is attendance at home games?	
14. How do you travel? Bus? Vans? Plane?	
15. Do you have team rules? Who enforces them?	
16. Do you run a pre-season conditioning program? Summer?	
Financial Questions	
1. Are academic scholarships available? Do you combine academic/athletic money?	
2. Am I a scholarship caliber player?	
3. For what reason would I lose my scholarship?	

School Profile	Recruiting Checklist	Date Completed	Points Earned
School	Add School to your list – 10 pts.		
Nickname/Mascot	Learn about school – 10 pts.		
School Colors	Fill out team recruiting questionnaire 30 pts.		
Type of College	Send Intro Email – 50 pts.		
Enrollment	Get a reply from coach – 50 pts.		
Location	Create a Video – 100 pts.		
Setting	Be evaluated by coach – 100 pts.		
Miles from home	Schedule Campus Visit – 50 pts.		
Tuition	Visit campus – 100 pts.		
Avg. Net Cost	Meet with coaching staff – 50 pts.		
Student: Faculty Ratio	Stay overnight on campus – 50 pts.		
Avg. SAT/ACT Scores	Attend ID Camp/Clinic – 100 pts.		
Athletic Program	Ask coach where you stand – 100 pts.		
Division / Conference	Verbal commitment – 200 pts.		
Head Coach	Submit an application – 200 pts.		
Email Address/Phone #	Sign an NLI (DI and DII only) 300 pts.		
Assistant Coach	Get Accepted – 500 pts.		
Email Address/Phone #			
Current Roster Size	Total Points Possible – 2000 pts.		
Previous Season Record	Total Points Earned		
Conference Finish	Goal Range = 1000 – 1500 points		

Recruiting Activity	Date	Notes

College Checklist	Completed	Date	Notes
Campus Tour			
Ate in Dining Hall			
Visited Dormitory			
Visited Athletic Facilities			
Met Coaching Staff			
Stayed Overnight			
Attended a Class			
Met a Professor in your major			
Attended a Practice			
Attended a Game			
Attended a Camp/Clinic			
Submitted an Application			

ACADEMIC / MERIT SCHOLARSHIP OFFER: _____ **ATHLETIC SCHOLARSHIP OFFER:** _____

Types of Recruiting Activities   Unofficial Visit – Official Visit – Contact – Evaluation – Phone Call – Email – Text Message

Academic Questions	
1. Does the school offer my major?	
2. Is there academic support for student-athletes? Are there required study halls?	
3. Do student-athletes have priority class registration?	
4. Does the school offer summer programs?	
5. What percentage of graduates does the school place into the work force?	
6. What is the graduation rate of the team over the last five years?	
7. What is the attitude of the faculty towards student-athlete's?	
Social Questions	
1. What is male to female ratio?	
2. Do students leave campus for the weekend?	
3. What is on campus housing like? Freshmen? Sophomores? Upperclassmen?	
4. Is on campus housing guaranteed for all four years?	
5. As a student-athlete can I live off campus?	
6. Are there co-ed dorms?	
7. Is there student-athlete housing?	
8. How are the dining facilities? How is the meal plan set up?	

Athletic Questions	
1. What system does the coach play? Defensive? Attacking?	
2. What is your coaching philosophy?	
3. How many players does the team carry? How many players play per game? Travel squad?	
4. How many starters are returning? How many at my position?	
5. What position do you seem me playing in your system? When do you expect me to make an impact?	
6. What is the nature of the conference? Is there a conference tournament?	
7. What are the facilities like? Do you share the facility?	
8. What type of locker room facility do you have? Team Room?	
9. What type of weight room facilities are available?	
10. Do you have a strength and conditioning coach?	
11. Do you lift throughout the season or just in the off-season?	
12. What is your Non-Conference schedule like?	
13. What is attendance at home games?	
14. How do you travel? Bus? Vans? Plane?	
15. Do you have team rules? Who enforces them?	
16. Do you run a pre-season conditioning program? Summer?	
Financial Questions	
1. Are academic scholarships available? Do you combine academic/athletic money?	
2. Am I a scholarship caliber player?	
3. For what reason would I lose my scholarship?	

School Profile	Recruiting Checklist	Date Completed	Points Earned
School	Add School to your list – 10 pts.		
Nickname/Mascot	Learn about school – 10 pts.		
School Colors	Fill out team recruiting questionnaire 30 pts.		
Type of College	Send Intro Email – 50 pts.		
Enrollment	Get a reply from coach – 50 pts.		
Location	Create a Video – 100 pts.		
Setting	Be evaluated by coach – 100 pts.		
Miles from home	Schedule Campus Visit – 50 pts.		
Tuition	Visit campus – 100 pts.		
Avg. Net Cost	Meet with coaching staff – 50 pts.		
Student: Faculty Ratio	Stay overnight on campus – 50 pts.		
Avg. SAT/ACT Scores	Attend ID Camp/Clinic – 100 pts.		
Athletic Program	Ask coach where you stand – 100 pts.		
Division / Conference	Verbal commitment – 200 pts.		
Head Coach	Submit an application – 200 pts.		
Email Address/Phone #	Sign an NLI (DI and DII only) 300 pts.		
Assistant Coach	Get Accepted – 500 pts.		
Email Address/Phone #			
Current Roster Size	Total Points Possible – 2000 pts.		
Previous Season Record	Total Points Earned		
Conference Finish	Goal Range = 1000 – 1500 points		

Recruiting Activity	Date	Notes

College Checklist	Completed	Date	Notes
Campus Tour			
Ate in Dining Hall			
Visited Dormitory			
Visited Athletic Facilities			
Met Coaching Staff			
Stayed Overnight			
Attended a Class			
Met a Professor in your major			
Attended a Practice			
Attended a Game			
Attended a Camp/Clinic			
Submitted an Application			

ACADEMIC / MERIT SCHOLARSHIP OFFER: _____ ATHLETIC SCHOLARSHIP OFFER: _____

Types of Recruiting Activities   Unofficial Visit – Official Visit – Contact – Evaluation – Phone Call – Email – Text Message

Academic Questions	
1. Does the school offer my major?	
2. Is there academic support for student-athletes? Are there required study halls?	
3. Do student-athletes have priority class registration?	
4. Does the school offer summer programs?	
5. What percentage of graduates does the school place into the work force?	
6. What is the graduation rate of the team over the last five years?	
7. What is the attitude of the faculty towards student-athlete's?	
Social Questions	
1. What is male to female ratio?	
2. Do students leave campus for the weekend?	
3. What is on campus housing like? Freshmen? Sophomores? Upperclassmen?	
4. Is on campus housing guaranteed for all four years?	
5. As a student-athlete can I live off campus?	
6. Are there co-ed dorms?	
7. Is there student-athlete housing?	
8. How are the dining facilities? How is the meal plan set up?	

The Top 3 Things I like about this school:

1. _____

2. _____

3. _____

Athletic Questions	
1. What system does the coach play? Defensive? Attacking?	
2. What is your coaching philosophy?	
3. How many players does the team carry? How many players play per game? Travel squad?	
4. How many starters are returning? How many at my position?	
5. What position do you seem me playing in your system? When do you expect me to make an impact?	
6. What is the nature of the conference? Is there a conference tournament?	
7. What are the facilities like? Do you share the facility?	
8. What type of locker room facility do you have? Team Room?	
9. What type of weight room facilities are available?	
10. Do you have a strength and conditioning coach?	
11. Do you lift throughout the season or just in the off-season?	
12. What is your Non-Conference schedule like?	
13. What is attendance at home games?	
14. How do you travel? Bus? Vans? Plane?	
15. Do you have team rules? Who enforces them?	
16. Do you run a pre-season conditioning program? Summer?	
Financial Questions	
1. Are academic scholarships available? Do you combine academic/athletic money?	
2. Am I a scholarship caliber player?	
3. For what reason would I lose my scholarship?	

School Profile		Recruiting Checklist	Date Completed	Points Earned
School		Add School to your list – 10 pts.		
Nickname/Mascot		Learn about school – 10 pts.		
School Colors		Fill out team recruiting questionnaire 30 pts.		
Type of College		Send Intro Email – 50 pts.		
Enrollment		Get a reply from coach – 50 pts.		
Location		Create a Video – 100 pts.		
Setting		Be evaluated by coach – 100 pts.		
Miles from home		Schedule Campus Visit – 50 pts.		
Tuition		Visit campus – 100 pts.		
Avg. Net Cost		Meet with coaching staff – 50 pts.		
Student: Faculty Ratio		Stay overnight on campus – 50 pts.		
Avg. SAT/ACT Scores		Attend ID Camp/Clinic – 100 pts.		
Athletic Program		Ask coach where you stand – 100 pts.		
Division / Conference		Verbal commitment – 200 pts.		
Head Coach		Submit an application – 200 pts.		
Email Address/Phone #		Sign an NLI (DI and DII only) 300 pts.		
Assistant Coach		Get Accepted – 500 pts.		
Email Address/Phone #				
Current Roster Size		Total Points Possible – 2000 pts.		
Previous Season Record		Total Points Earned		
Conference Finish		Goal Range = 1000 – 1500 points		

152 | Page   Guiding Future Stars to Gaining Future Success

Recruiting Activity	Date	Notes

College Checklist	Completed	Date	Notes
Campus Tour			
Ate in Dining Hall			
Visited Dormitory			
Visited Athletic Facilities			
Met Coaching Staff			
Stayed Overnight			
Attended a Class			
Met a Professor in your major			
Attended a Practice			
Attended a Game			
Attended a Camp/Clinic			
Submitted an Application			

ACADEMIC / MERIT SCHOLARSHIP OFFER: _____ **ATHLETIC SCHOLARSHIP OFFER:** _____

Types of Recruiting Activities   Unofficial Visit – Official Visit – Contact – Evaluation – Phone Call – Email – Text Message

Academic Questions	
1. Does the school offer my major?	
2. Is there academic support for student-athletes? Are there required study halls?	
3. Do student-athletes have priority class registration?	
4. Does the school offer summer programs?	
5. What percentage of graduates does the school place into the work force?	
6. What is the graduation rate of the team over the last five years?	
7. What is the attitude of the faculty towards student-athlete's?	
Social Questions	
1. What is male to female ratio?	
2. Do students leave campus for the weekend?	
3. What is on campus housing like? Freshmen? Sophomores? Upperclassmen?	
4. Is on campus housing guaranteed for all four years?	
5. As a student-athlete can I live off campus?	
6. Are there co-ed dorms?	
7. Is there student-athlete housing?	
8. How are the dining facilities? How is the meal plan set up?	

The Top 3 Things I like about this school:

1. _____

2. _____

3. _____

Athletic Questions	
1. What system does the coach play? Defensive? Attacking?	
2. What is your coaching philosophy?	
3. How many players does the team carry? How many players play per game? Travel squad?	
4. How many starters are returning? How many at my position?	
5. What position do you seem me playing in your system? When do you expect me to make an impact?	
6. What is the nature of the conference? Is there a conference tournament?	
7. What are the facilities like? Do you share the facility?	
8. What type of locker room facility do you have? Team Room?	
9. What type of weight room facilities are available?	
10. Do you have a strength and conditioning coach?	
11. Do you lift throughout the season or just in the off-season?	
12. What is your Non-Conference schedule like?	
13. What is attendance at home games?	
14. How do you travel? Bus? Vans? Plane?	
15. Do you have team rules? Who enforces them?	
16. Do you run a pre-season conditioning program? Summer?	
Financial Questions	
1. Are academic scholarships available? Do you combine academic/athletic money?	
2. Am I a scholarship caliber player?	
3. For what reason would I lose my scholarship?	

ONLINE RESOURCES FOR STUDENT-ATHLETES

NCAA	www.ncaa.org
NCAA Eligibility Center	www.eligibilitycenter.org
NAIA	www.naia.com
National Consortium Academics and Sports	www.ncasports.org
NCAA Sports	www.ncaasports.com

FINANCIAL AND EDUCATIONAL RESOURCES WEBSITES

www.fafsa.ed.gov

www.athleticscholarships.com

www.scholarshipstats.com/ncaalimits.html

www.collegeboard.org

http://nces.ed.gov/collegenavigator/

www.collegeview.com

www.princetonreview.com

CONTRIBUTORS

TJ Burns - Strength and Conditioning Coach, Launch Sports Performance
www.launchsp.com

Ryan Defibaugh - MA in Sports Administration, MA in Counseling

Tom Gosselin - Head Women's Soccer Coach; Mount St. Mary's University
www.mountathletics.com

Greg White – Founder, Greg White Speaks: *50 Questions Every Student-Athlete Should Answer before Committing to a School*

www.gregwhitespeaks.com

COLLEGE COACHES BIOS

Jamion Christian, Head Men's Basketball Coach Mount St. Mary's University

- 3rd season as Head Basketball Coach at Mount St. Mary's
- Led team to the 2014 NCAA Tournament
- Previously coached at Emory and Henry, Bucknell, William and Mary, and Virginia Commonwealth.

Lindsey Munday, Head Women's Lacrosse Coach University of Southern California

- 3rd season as Head Women's Lacrosse Coach at USC
- Previously coached at Northwestern and Mount St. Mary's
- Member of the US Women's National Lacrosse Team
- 2 Time FIL World Cup Champion
- 5 Time NCAA Champion with Northwestern
- Lacrosse Magazine's 2013 Person of the Year

Paul Royal, Head Women's Soccer Coach LaSalle University

- 11th season as Head Women's Soccer Coach at LaSalle
- Programs all times win leader
- Led the Explorers to 4 consecutive NCAA appearances
- 2 x A10 Coach of the Year
- 2 x A10 Conference Championships
- Member of the US Soccer National Training Center Staff

Pat Horvath, Head Baseball Coach Philadelphia University

- 5th season as Head Baseball Coach at Philadelphia University
- Previously coached at Rider University, Texas A&M Corpus Christi, and Palm Beach Atlantic University.

Jessica Wolverton, Head Women's Volleyball Coach McDaniel College

- 3rd season as Head Volleyball Coach at McDaniel College
- Previously coached at Sewanee and a short stint at Florida St.
- Attended Gettysburg College where she was the 2003 Centennial Conference Player of the Year.

Jill Calloway, Former Assistant Softball Coach, University of Maryland

- Founder and Owner of 5 Star Athletics
- Played at the University of Maryland
- Recruiting Coordinator 2013 – 2014 season

REFERENCES

Benjamin, Ashley B. Cauthen, Michael, and Donnelly, Patrick. *The Student-Athlete's College Recruitment Guide.* New York: Ferguson, 2009. Print

Brown, Kerry. "The Walk-On Guide for College Athletes - NCSA Athletic Recruiting Blog." *NCSA Athletic Recruiting Blog.* NCSA Sports, 14 Feb. 2013. Web. 16 Dec. 2014.

Brown, Kerry. "20 Questions to Expect from a College Coach" *NCSA Athletic Recruiting Blog.* NCSA Sports, 14 Feb. 2013. Web 16 Dec. 2014

Brown, Kerry (2012) *"Top 50 Recruiting Tips –* NCSA Athletic Recruiting Blog"NCSA Athletic Recruiting Blog. NCSA Sports, 09 Sept. 2012 Web. 16 Dec 2014.

Brown, Stewart. *The Student-Athlete's Guide to Getting Recruited: How to Win Scholarships, Attract Colleges and Excel as an Athlete.* Chicago: SuperCollege, LLC, 2012 Print

Burnsed, Brian (2010*) 9 Tips for SAT Success.* US News and World Report

Lohrbeer, Trevor. *How to Create an Effective Weighted Pro Con Lis*t. Lean Decisions
http://leandecisions.com/2012/09/how-to-create-an-effective-weighted-pro-con-list.html

Social Media Coach for Athletes (2012) *College Athlete Twitter Tips to Live By*
http://socialmediacoachforathletes.com/college-athlete-twitter-tips-to-live-by/

O'Brien, Steve. *Student-Athlete Guide to Be Recruited.* Goal: College Athlete

Tarter, Barry. "Three E's of Exposure – *EXACT Sports."* 25 Sept. 2013. Web 16 Dec 2014

Guiding Future Stars College Recruiting Education

GFS wants to help educate prospective student-athletes and their families about the college recruiting process so they can make informed decisions to find the right school to fit their academic, athletic, and personal needs. The GFS approach to the college recruiting process is all about educating prospective student-athletes about the importance of finding the school where they will have the best college experience.

GFS helps share this message through its college recruiting education programs such as the College Recruiting Playbook, college recruiting seminars and workshops, student-athlete guidance programs, and the exposure and education initiative.

College Recruiting X's and O's Seminar - The Recruiting X's and O's seminar is designed to educate prospective student-athletes, parents, coaches, and administrators about the college recruiting process. The presentation will discuss the benefits of playing sports in college and what attributes college coaches look for in recruits. GFS will also provide a thorough overview of the 5 phases of the college recruiting process
- Planning and Preparation
- Communication
- Gaining Exposure
- Decision Making
- Beyond the Decision

Topics College Recruiting X's and O's Seminar will cover

- NCAA Eligibility Center and NCAA Rules and Regulations
- How to build a balanced list of schools
- The differences between DI, DII, DIII, and NAIA schools
- Communicating with college coaches
- Gaining Exposure
- Scholarships, Financial Aid, and Admissions Process

College Recruiting Workshops - The Recruiting workshops are a hands on approach to navigate through the recruiting process. They are designed to assist prospective student-athletes work through certain phases of the college recruiting process in a small group setting utilizing the college recruiting playbook and other resources. There are a number of different workshops for prospective student-athletes depending on the grade of the student.

- Introduction to College Sports Workshop
- Planning, Preparation, and Communication Workshop
- Communication and Gaining Exposure Workshop
- Unofficial Visit and Overnight Visit Prep Workshop
- Decision Making Workshop
- Beyond the Decision Workshop
- Goal Setting and Time Management Workshop

Student-Athlete Success Playbook Coming Soon

You have decided on a college. Now What? It's time to prepare academically and athletically for the next four years of your life. What do you need to do to be a successful student-athlete? What do you need to know to be a successful student-athlete? The Guiding Future Stars Student-Athlete Success Playbook is a step by step guide to making the most out of your college "experience." This guide will tackle a number of issues that college student-athletes deal with every day.

- How to prepare athletically for your first year?
- How to set goals? How to manage your time wisely?
- How to prepare academically? What type of learner are you?
- Writing for Success in college
- How to communicate effectively? How to resolve conflict?
- How to live a healthy lifestyle in college?
- Managing Money
- Planning a Career
- And much more

Career Development Playbook Coming Soon

It's time to start thinking about life after college. What's your passion? Do you have a career in mind? Are you going to continue your education? The Guiding Future Stars Career Development Playbook will help you answer some of these questions. The Career Development Playbook will focus on a number of topics that will help guide you to a successful career.

- Identify skills and interests that pertain to selecting a career
- Develop personal career goals
- Research and choosing a career path
- Research and analyze graduate school options
- Write a comprehensive career plan
- Building your resume and cover letter
- Creating your network
- Interview Prep
- Acquiring an internship
- And much more

Journal Notes

ABOUT THE AUTHOR

Christopher J. Stack is the founder and president of Guiding Future Stars, a student-athlete development company that transforms high school players into excellent students, great athletes, and extraordinary people.

A former Division I soccer player for Mount St. Mary's University, he holds a degree in sports management and an MBA in marketing. Stack has worked in intercollegiate athletics for over twelve years. Starting his career in college administration at his alma mater as the coordinator of intramurals, he also served as the head assistant coach and recruiting coordinator for the university's women's soccer team. He eventually transitioned to the academic side of college sports as the coordinator of student-athlete academic support.

Stack now enjoys using his higher education experience to help high school students achieve their dreams of playing sports in college while also gaining first-rate educations.

FOLLOW GFS ON TWITTER @GUIDFUTURESTARS

LIKE US ON FACEBOOK: GUIDING FUTURE STARS

www.GuidingFutureStars.com